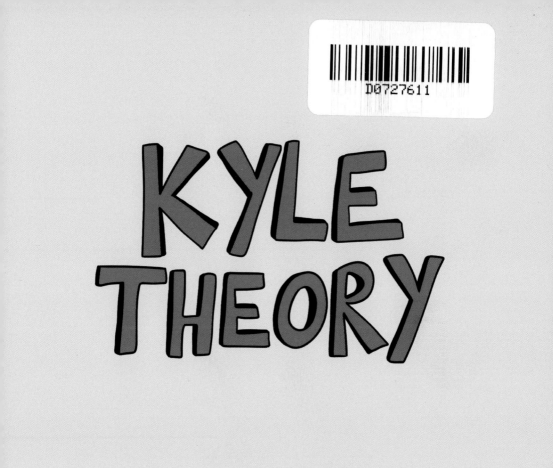

KYLE THEORY

LiLY O'FARRELL

KYLE THEORY

a book of @VULGADRAWINGS

THE

INDIGO

PRESS

THE INDIGO PRESS
50 Albemarle Street
London W1S 4BD
www.theindigopress.com

The Indigo Press Publishing Limited Re. No. 10995574
Registered Office: Wellesley House, Duke of Wellington Avenue,
Royal Arsenal, London SE18 6SS

ISBN 978-1-911648-30-7
eBook ISBN 978-1-911648-31-4

This edition first published in Great Britain in 2021 by The Indigo Press
Lily O'Farrell assets the moral right to be identified as the author of this work in accordance with
the Copyright, Designs and Patents Act 1988
First published in Great Britain in 2021 by The Indigo Press

A CIP catalogue record for this title is available from the British Library.

Design by James Nunn
Printed and bound in Great Britain by TJ Books Limited, Padstow

INTRODUCTION

Hello! Thank you for buying my book.

Three years ago I started drawing cartoons on the back of receipts at the restaurant I was working at. I was 21 and was starting to find that with every year that passed, the sexism I encountered became more transparent, more aggressive and less afraid of the consequences. Drawing and writing jokes about this was cathartic, and I started to upload my cartoons to Instagram where slowly my audience grew. To my surprise, many other people found them cathartic too - because, of course, these were shared experiences. Three years later, I'm now drawing silly cartoons at my desk all day, every day. I have my followers to thank for you buying this book.

Often sexism exists in the form of the occasional comments, the unspoken attitudes and the eye-rolls that build up day by day. It's hard to explain why they affect us so much, but it feels like a small leak that eventually fills up an entire swimming pool. Those are the acts of sexism that I've tried to depict in cartoon form, so you can have that lightbulb moment where you realize exactly what it was that bothered you about that guy you met at that awful gig in the basement of a dingy bar somewhere. This book is *Where's Wally?* but for everyday sexism.

The next 120 pages are a mixture of cartoons I've created throughout the last three years, and some new cartoons just for you. I hope you relate to what I've drawn, I hope you discover something new, I hope it makes you feel less alone, and most of all, I hope it makes you laugh.

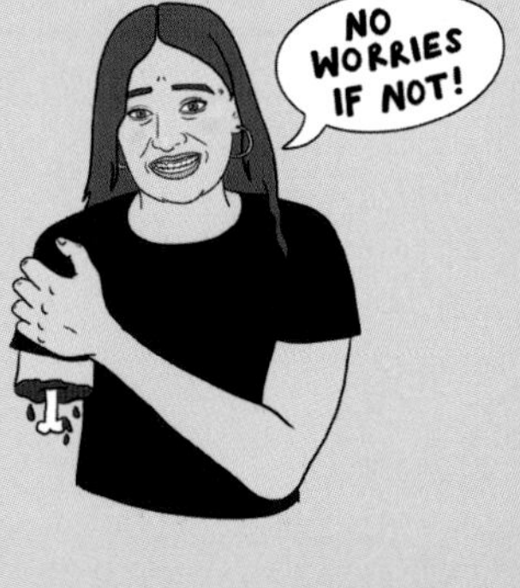
NO WORRIES IF NOT!

AAAAAND
DONE.
FEMINISM
This is a personal attack on me!
POSTING TO INSTAGRAM...
LOADING

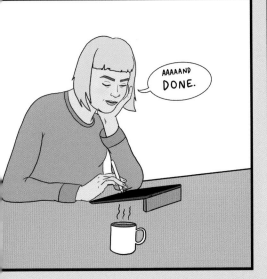

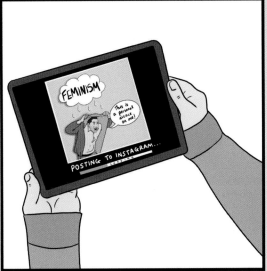

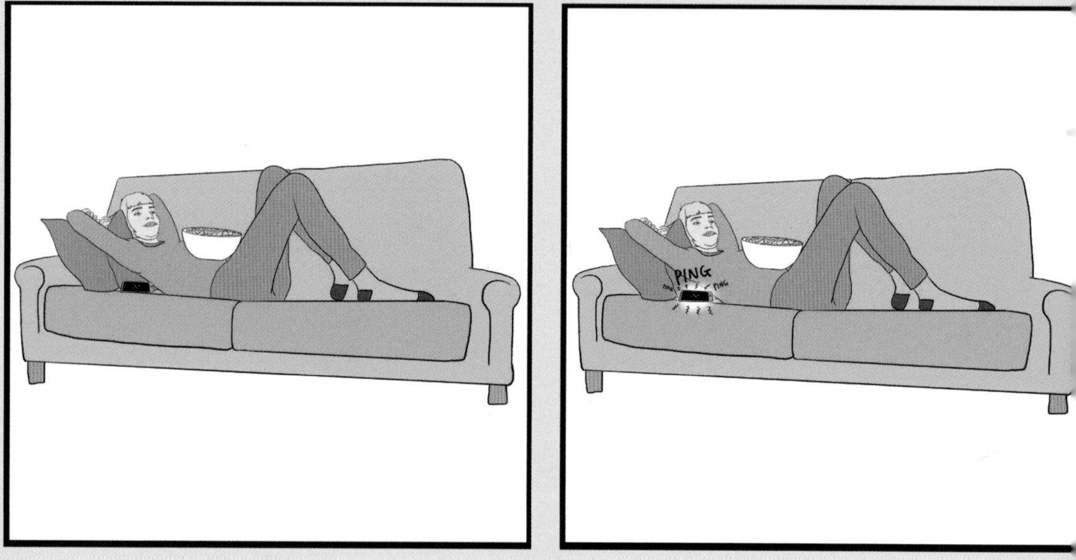
PING
PING

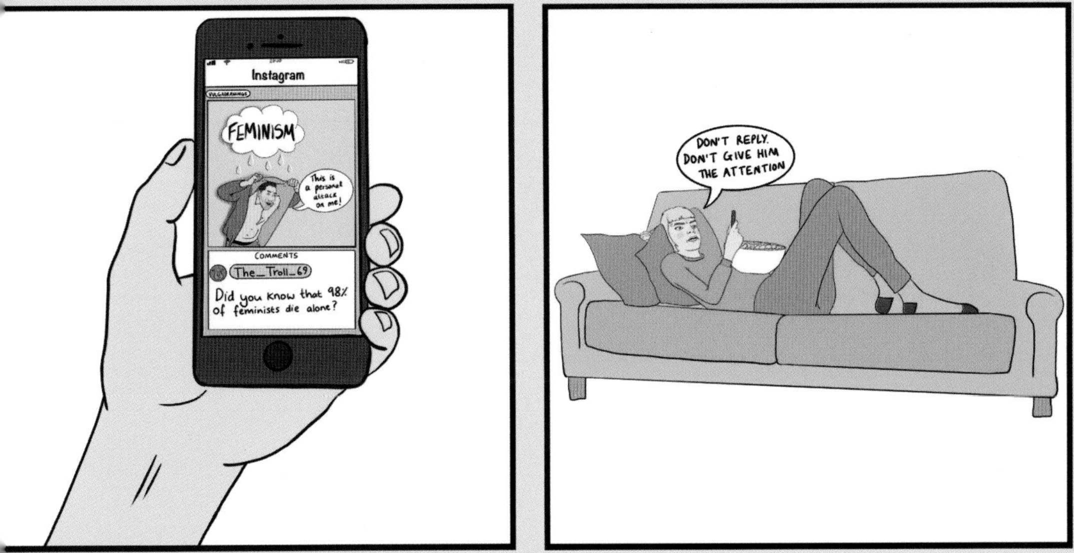
Instagram
FEMINISM
This is a personal attack on me!
COMMENTS
The_Troll_69
Did you know that 98% of feminists die alone?
DON'T REPLY. DON'T GIVE HIM THE ATTENTION

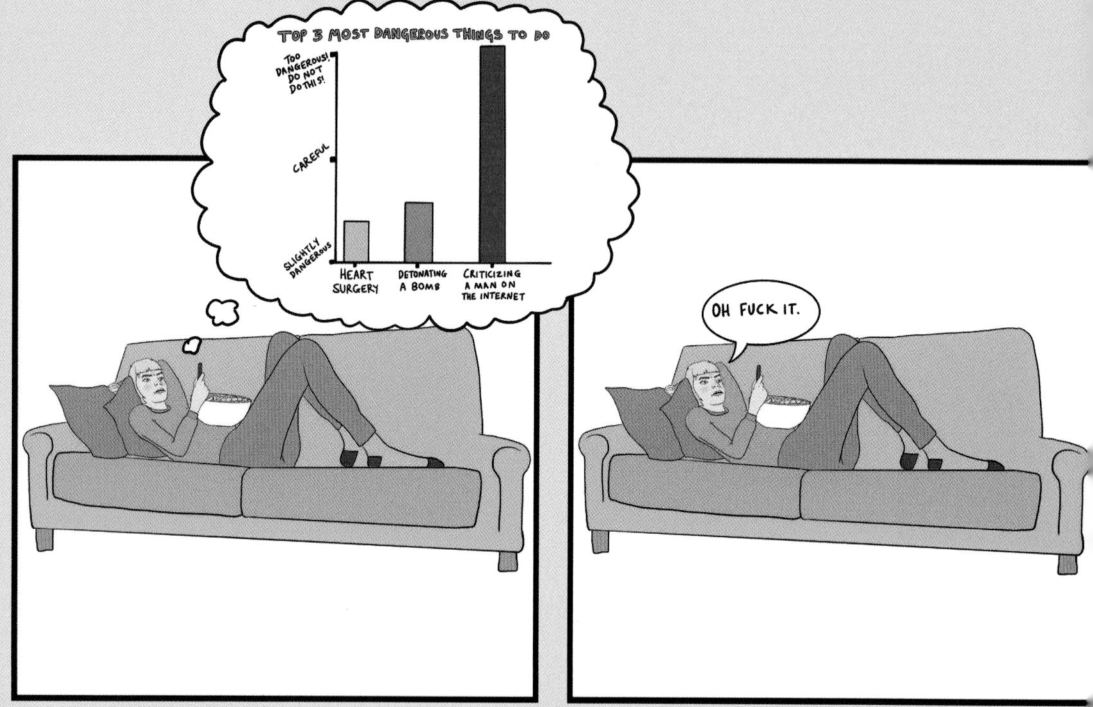
TOP 3 MOST DANGEROUS THINGS TO DO
TOO DANGEROUS! DO NOT DO THIS!
CAREFUL
SLIGHTLY DANGEROUS
HEART SURGERY
DETONATING A BOMB
CRITICIZING A MAN ON THE INTERNET
OH FUCK IT.

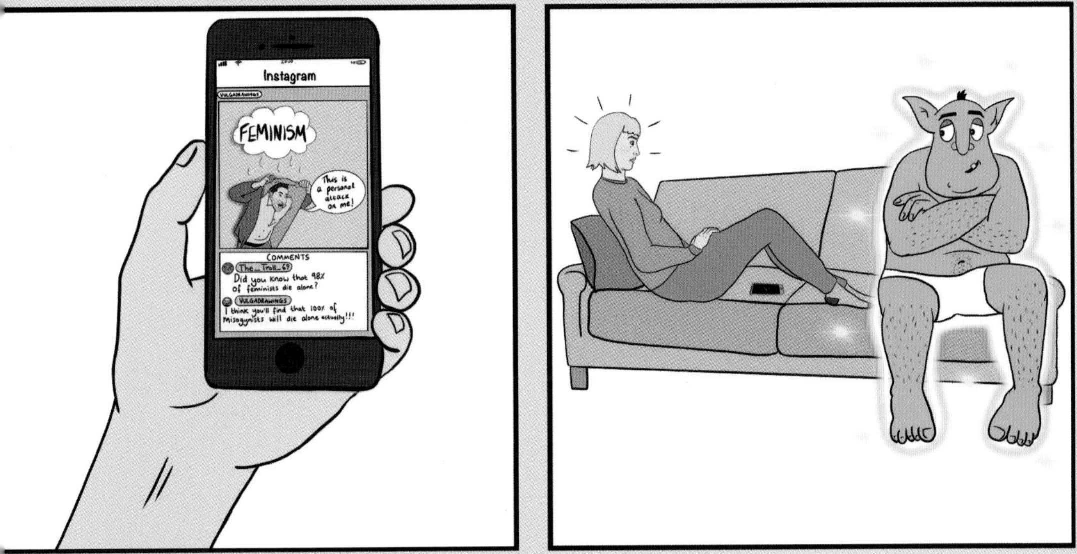
Instagram
VULGADRAWINGS
FEMINISM
This is a personal attack on me!
COMMENTS
The_Troll_69
Did you know that 98% of feminists die alone?
VULGADRAWINGS
I think you'll find that 100% of Misogynists will die alone actually!!!

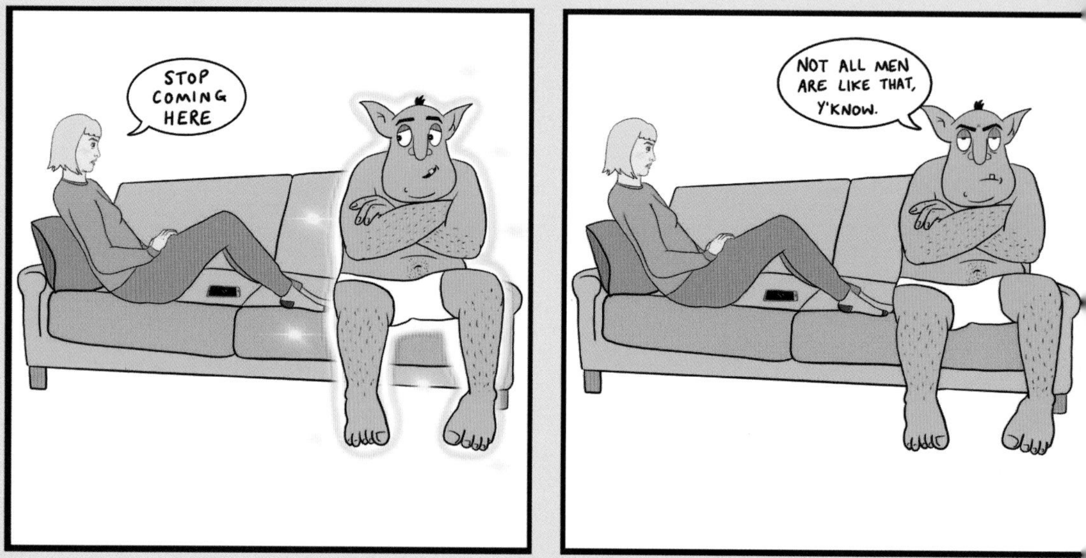
STOP COMING HERE
NOT ALL MEN ARE LIKE THAT, Y'KNOW.

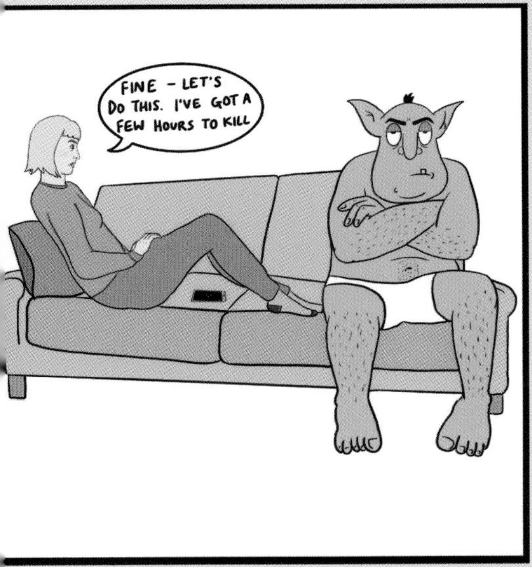
FINE - LET'S DO THIS. I'VE GOT A FEW HOURS TO KILL

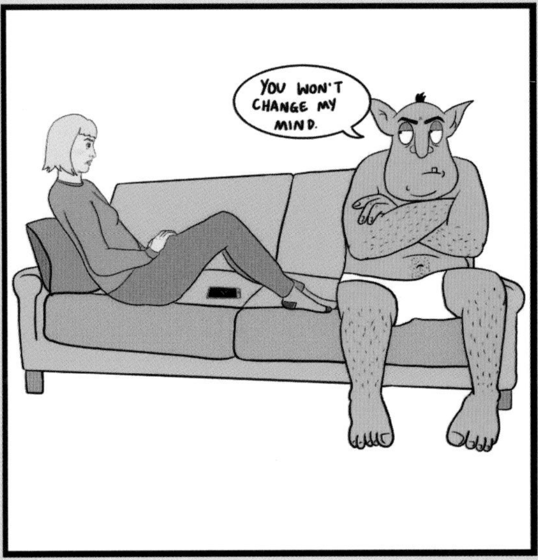
YOU WON'T CHANGE MY MIND.

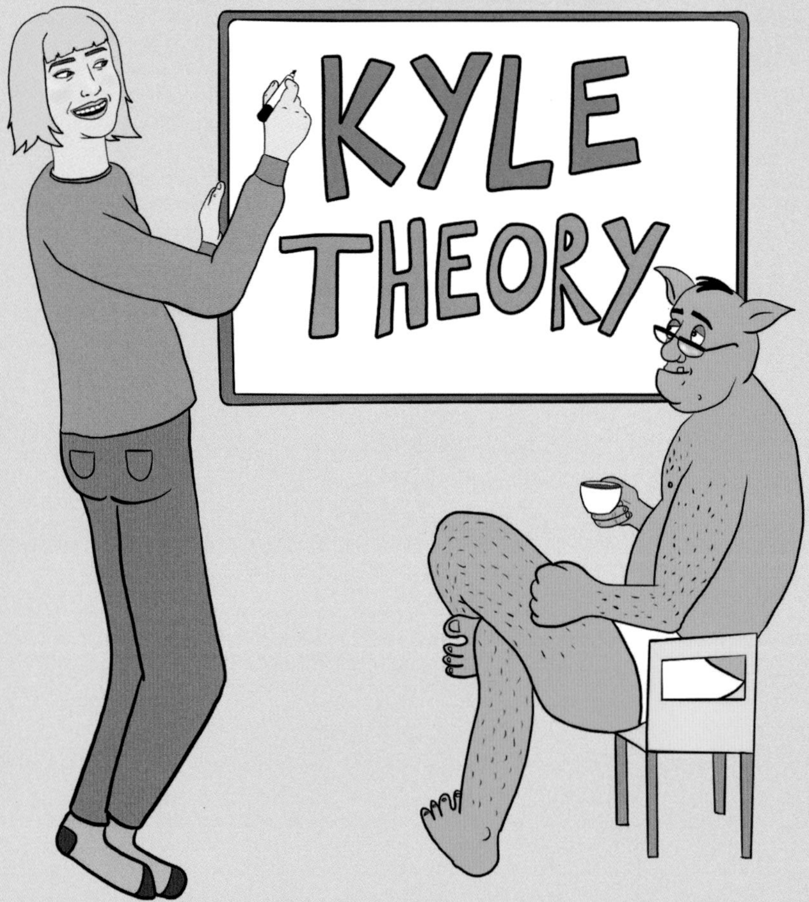
KYLE
THEORY

WHO IS KYLE?

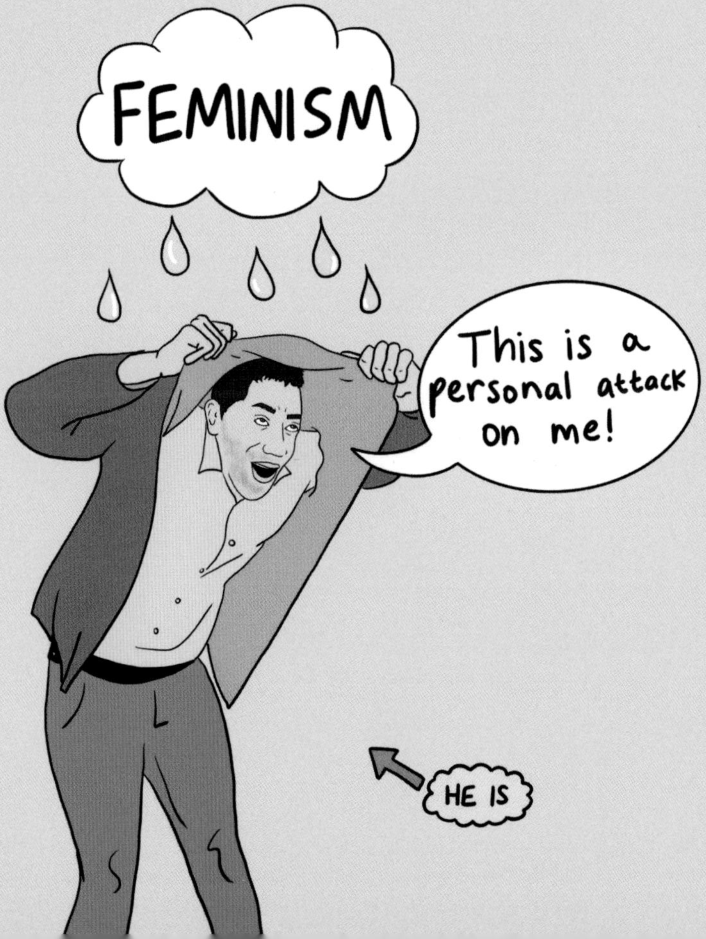
FEMINISM
This is a personal attack on me!
HE IS

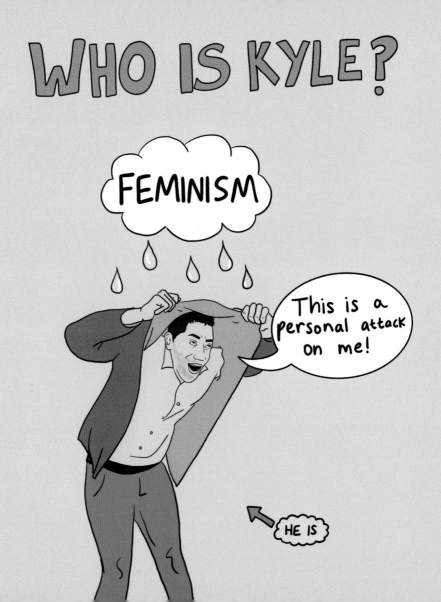

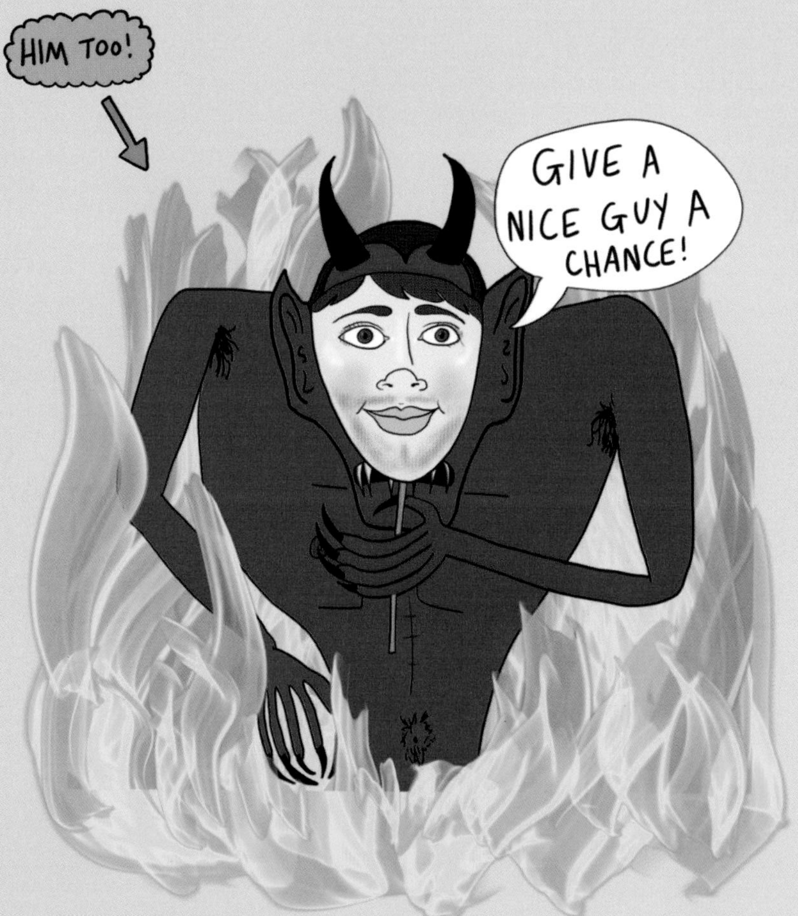
HIM TOO!
GIVE A NICE GUY A CHANCE!

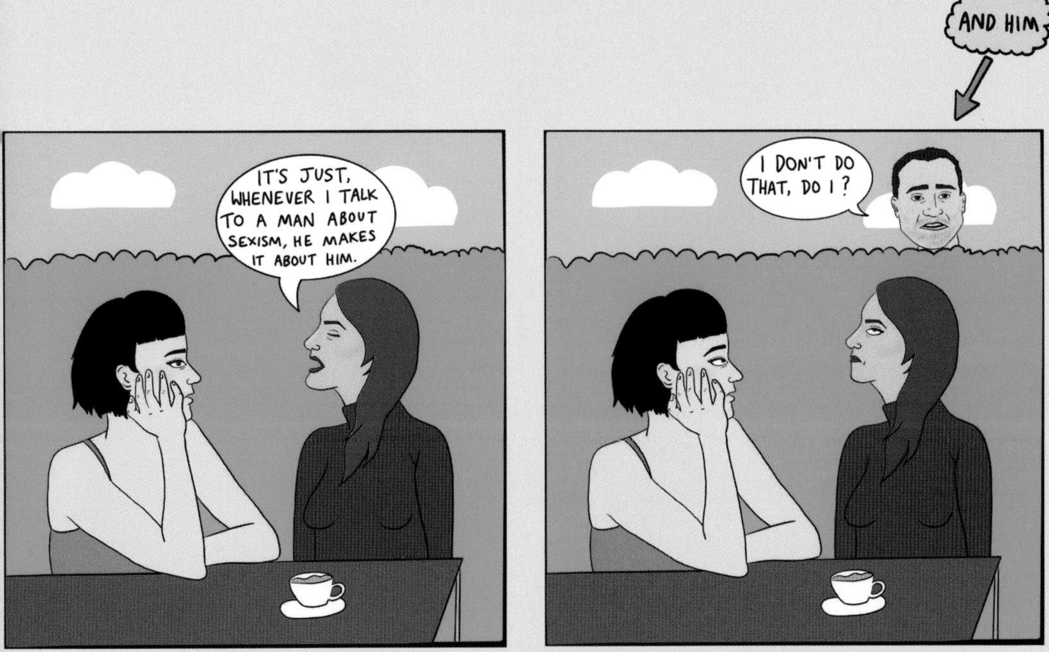
IT'S JUST, WHENEVER I TALK TO A MAN ABOUT SEXISM, HE MAKES IT ABOUT HIM.
AND HIM
I DON'T DO THAT, DO I?

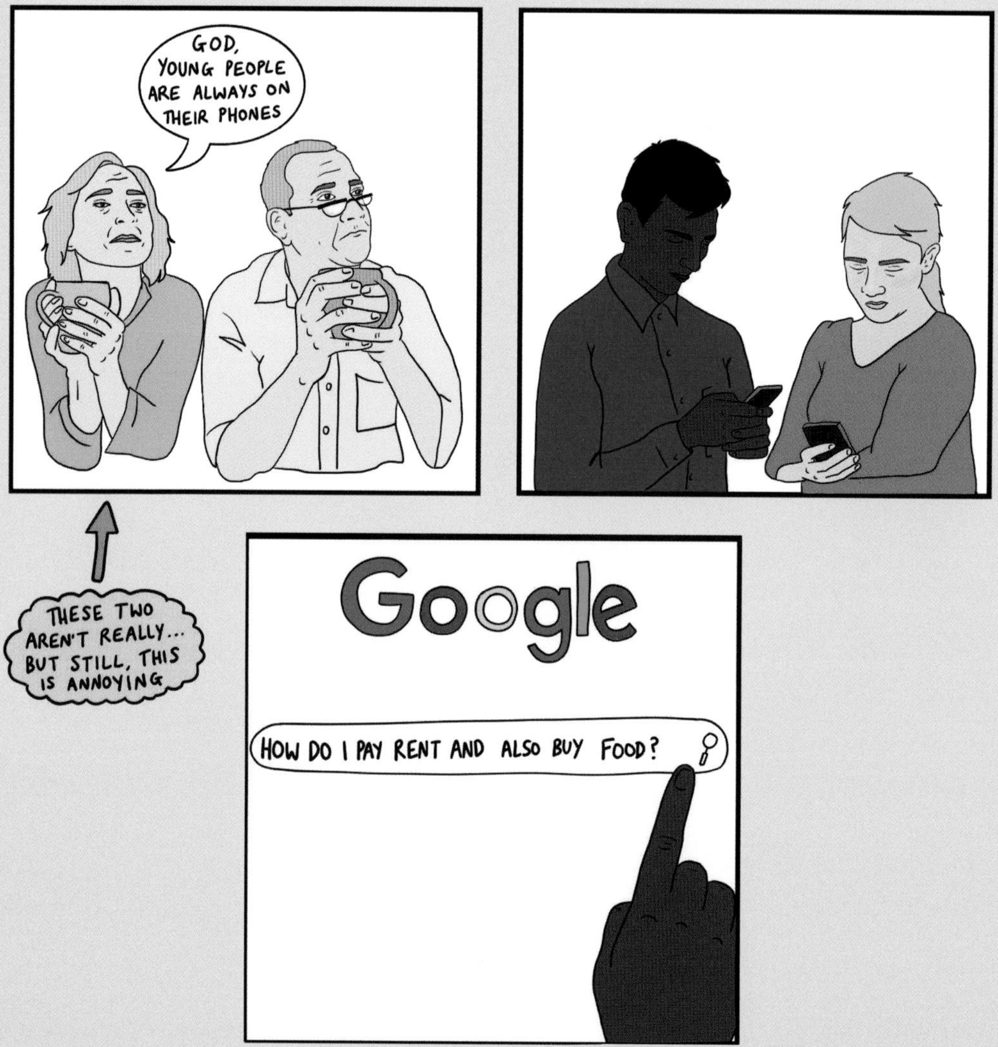
GOD, YOUNG PEOPLE ARE ALWAYS ON THEIR PHONES
THESE TWO AREN'T REALLY... BUT STILL, THIS IS ANNOYING
Google
HOW DO I PAY RENT AND ALSO BUY FOOD?

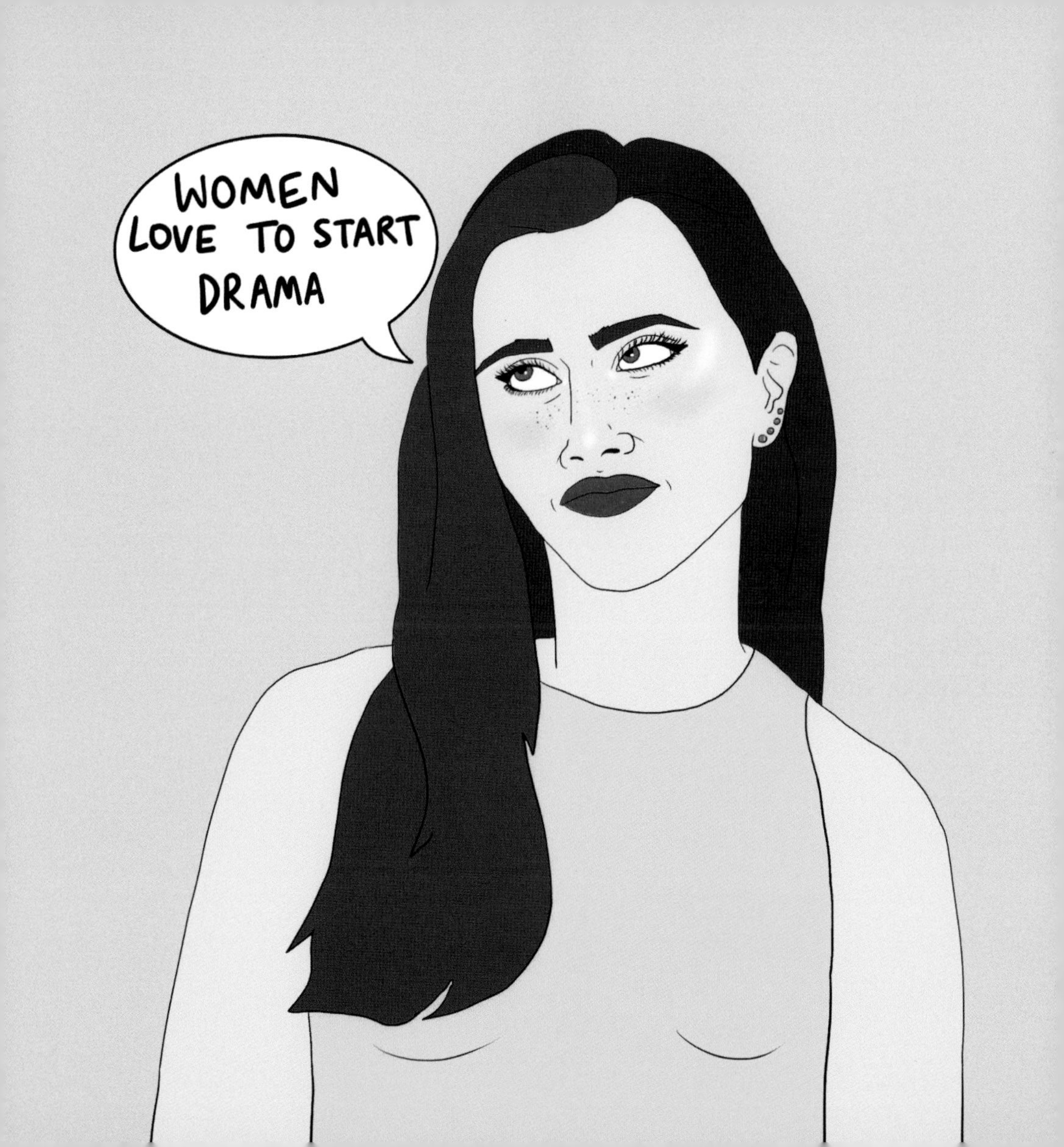
WOMEN LOVE TO START DRAMA

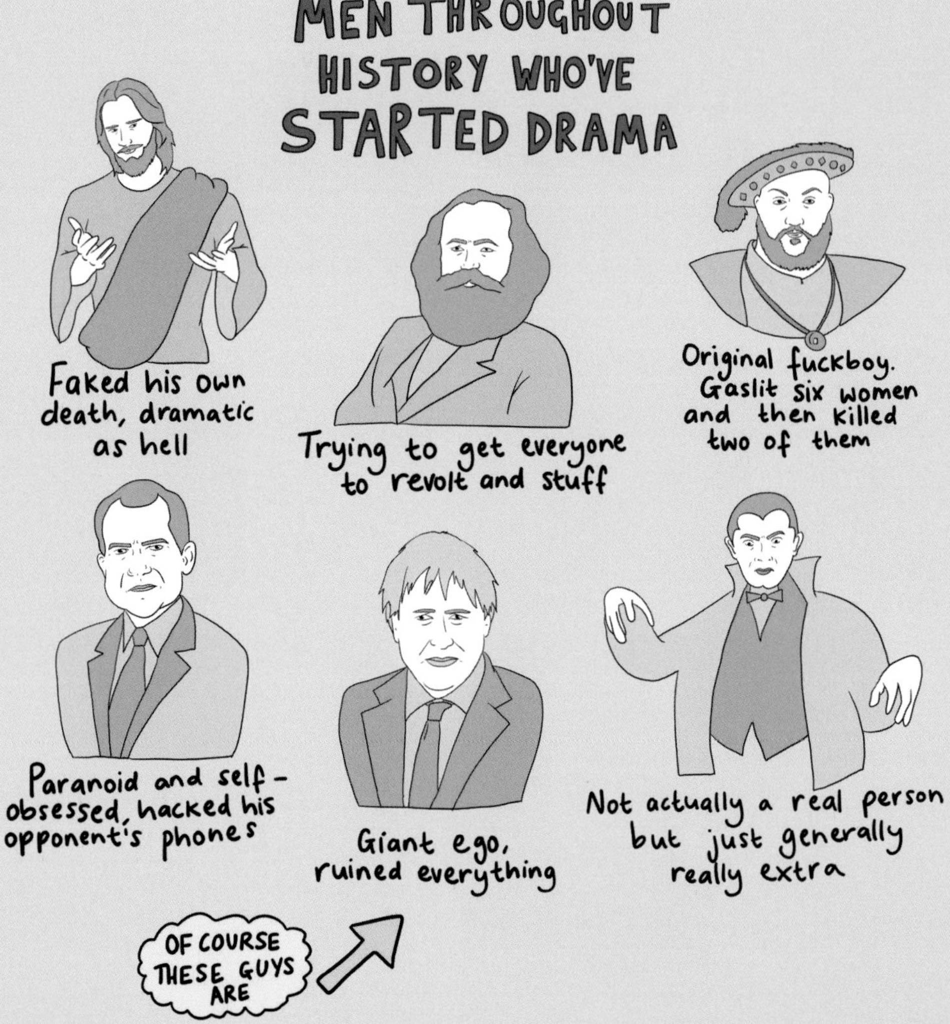
MEN THROUGHOUT HISTORY WHO'VE STARTED DRAMA
Faked his own death, dramatic as hell
Trying to get everyone to revolt and stuff
Original fuckboy. Gaslit six women and then killed two of them
Paranoid and self-obsessed, hacked his opponent's phones
Giant ego, ruined everything
Not actually a real person but just generally really extra
OF COURSE THESE GUYS ARE

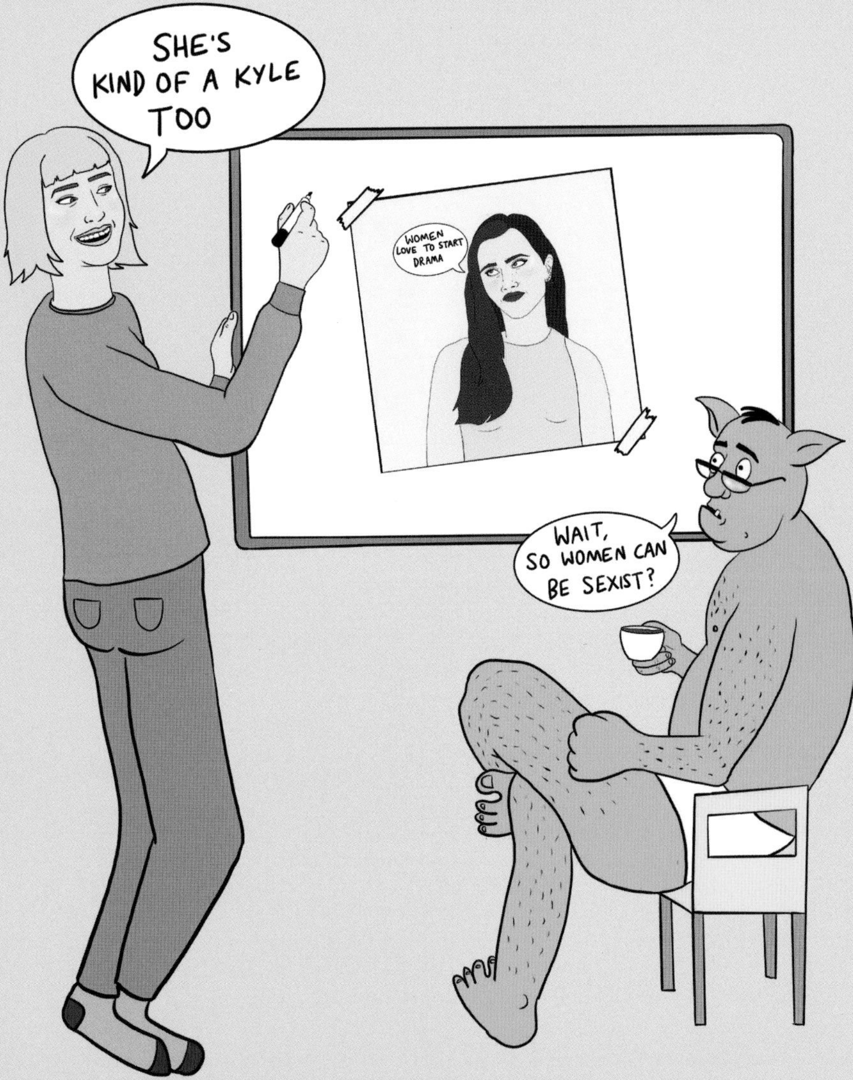
SHE'S KIND OF A KYLE TOO
WOMEN LOVE TO START DRAMA
WAIT, SO WOMEN CAN BE SEXIST?

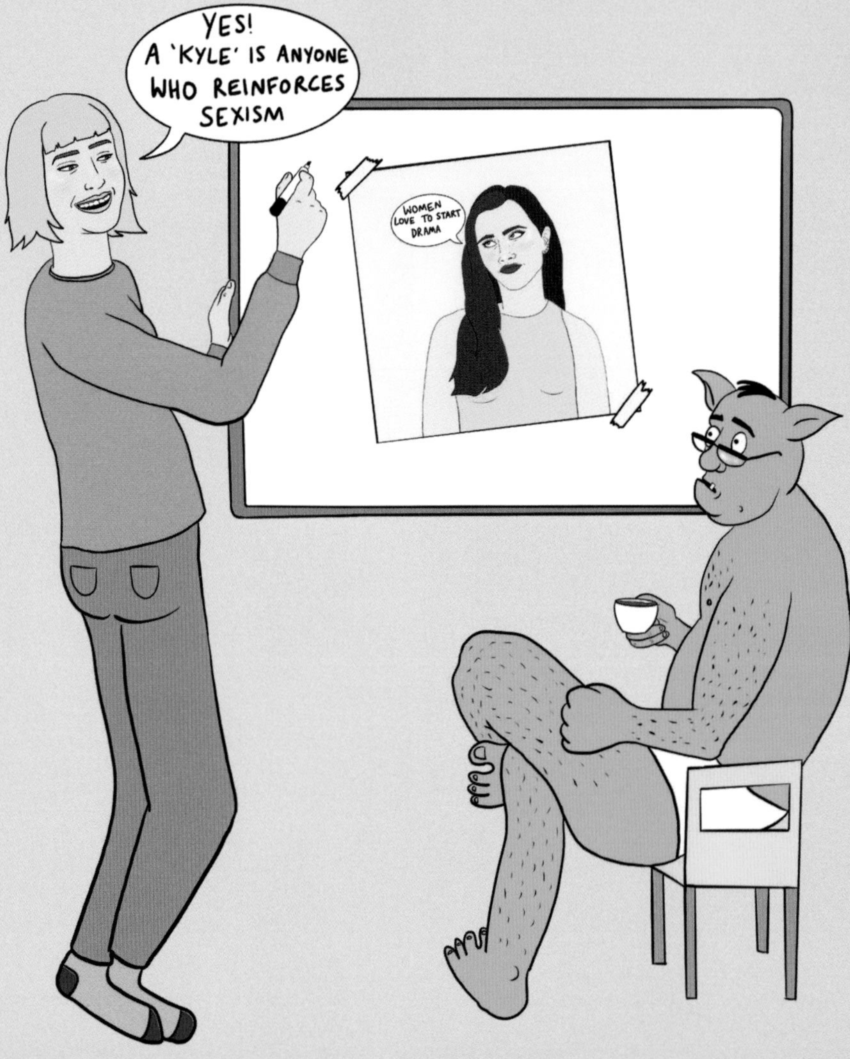
YES! A 'KYLE' IS ANYONE WHO REINFORCES SEXISM
WOMEN LOVE TO START DRAMA

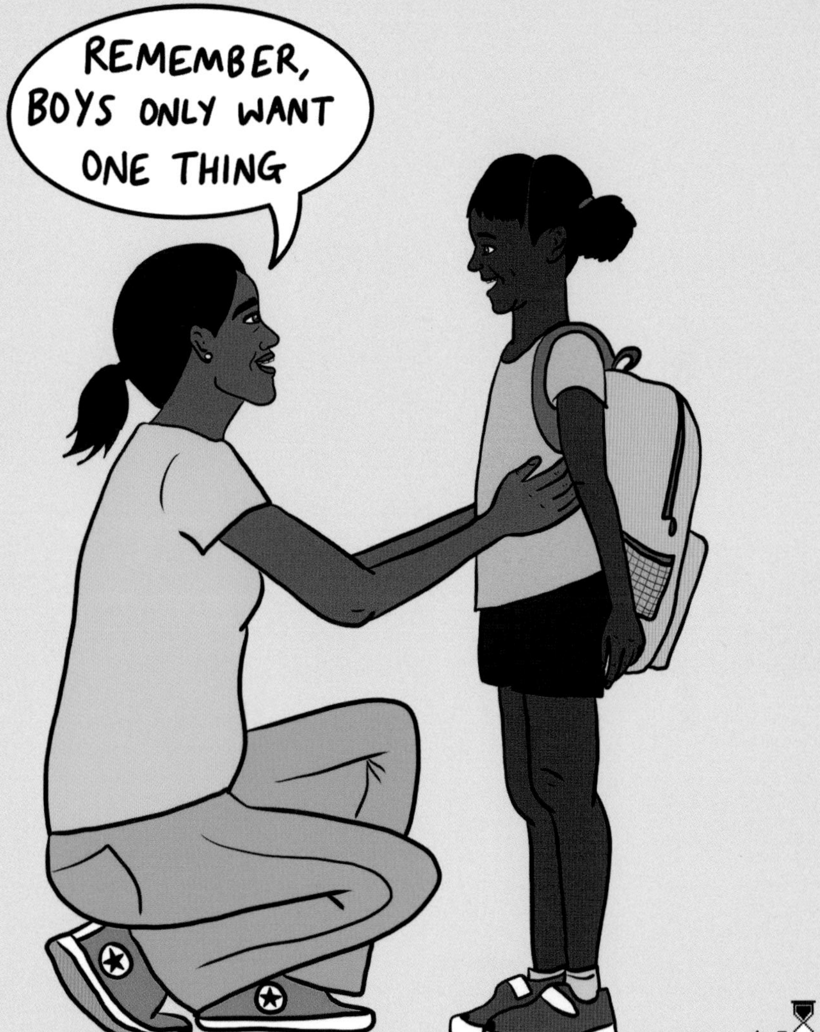
REMEMBER, BOYS ONLY WANT ONE THING
1 of 3

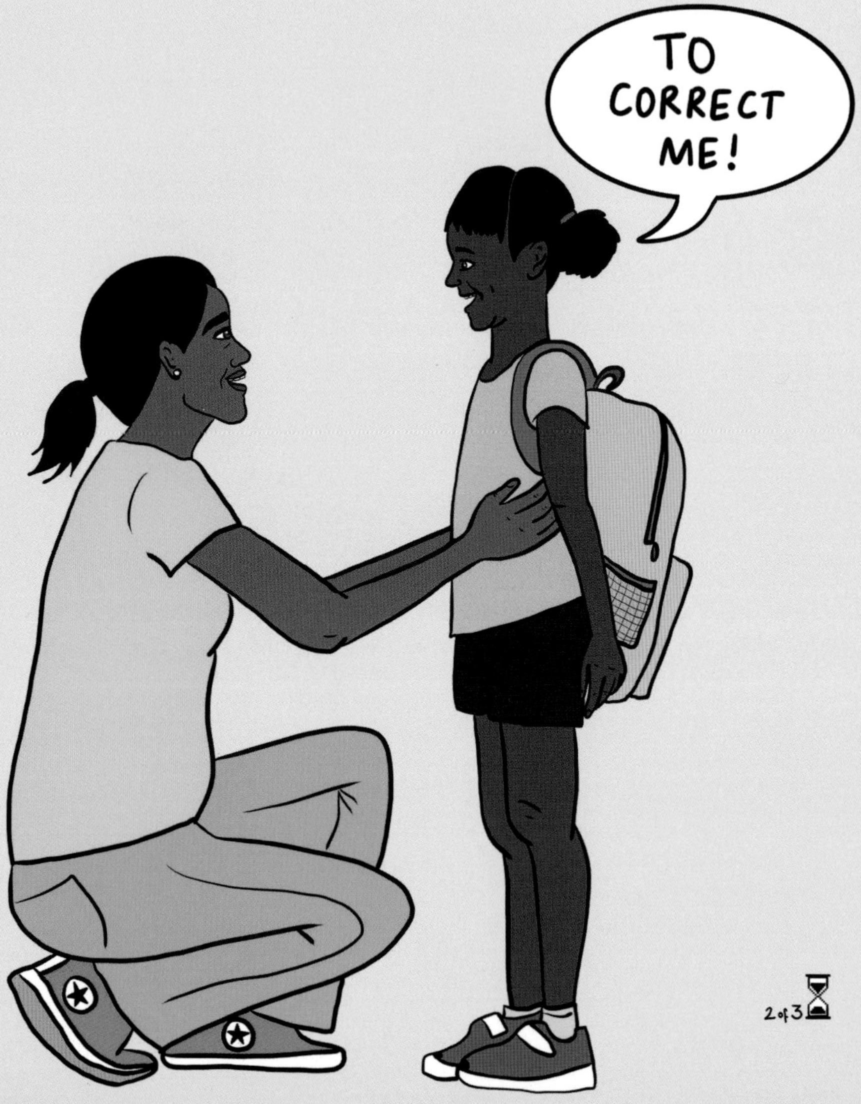
TO CORRECT ME!
2 of 3

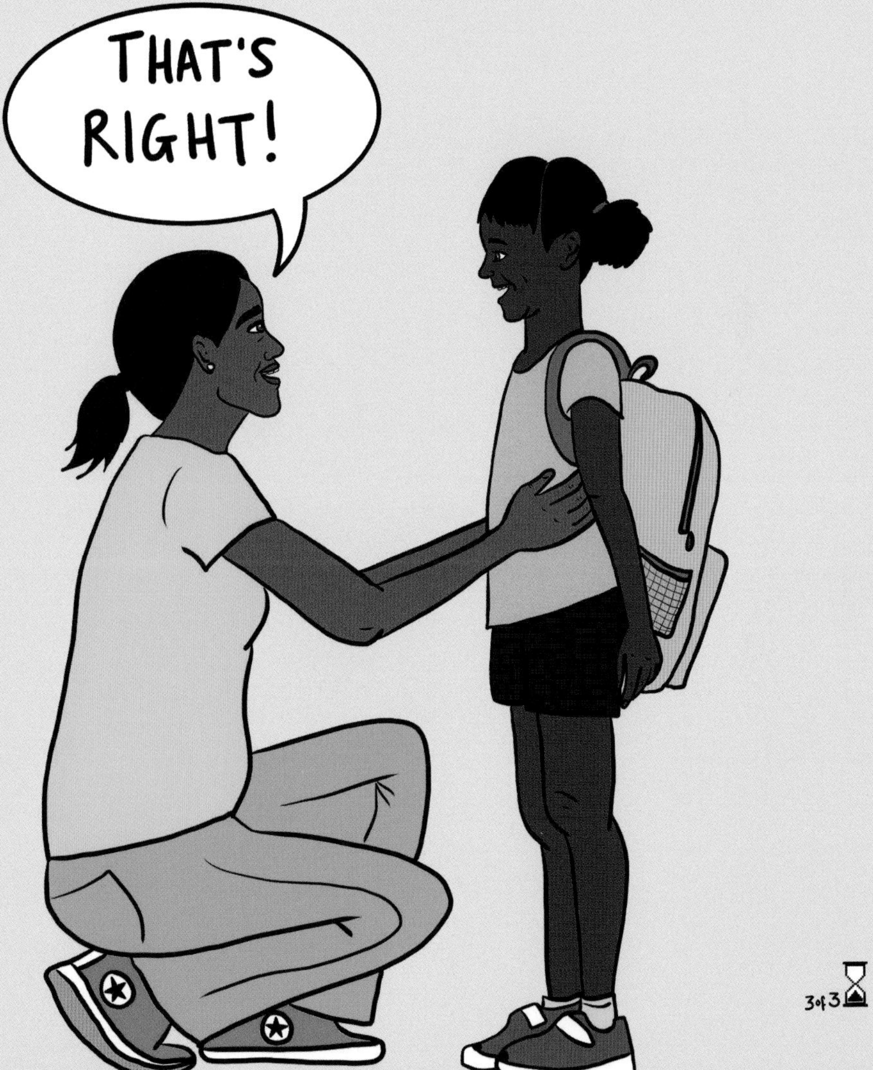
THAT'S RIGHT!
3of3

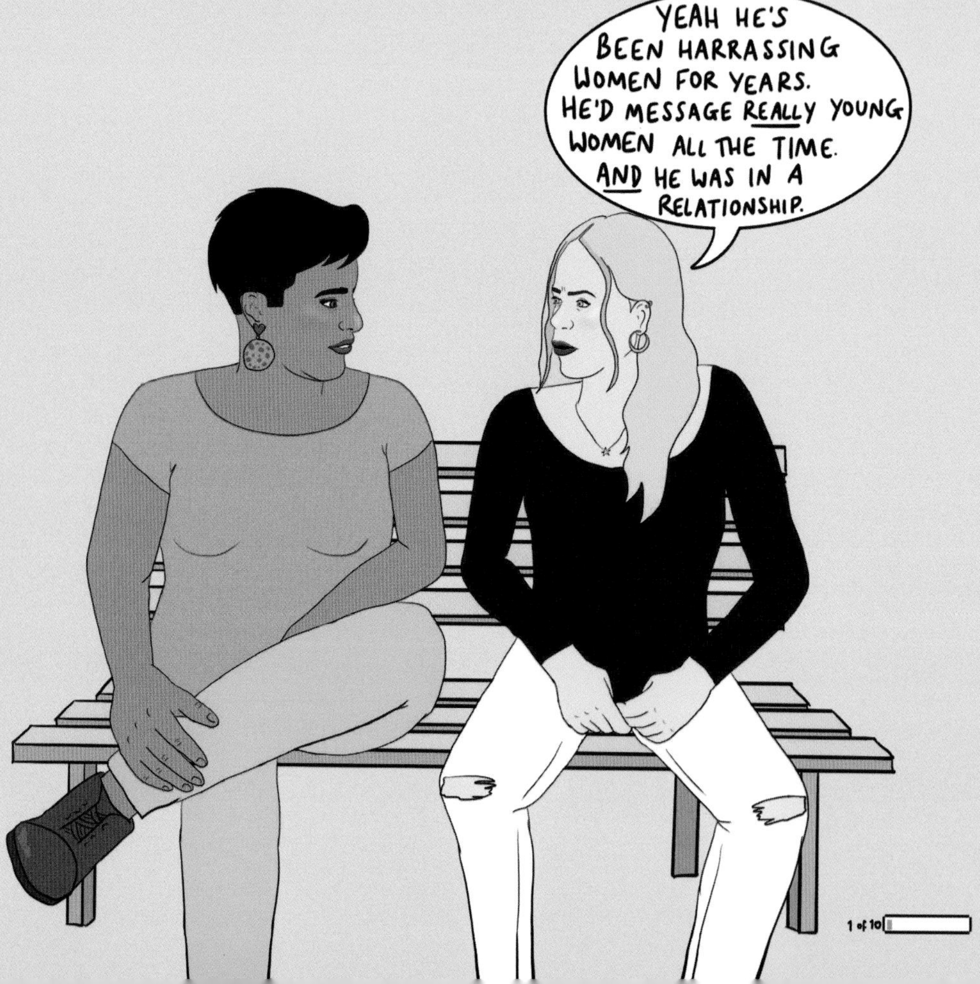
YEAH HE'S BEEN HARRASSING WOMEN FOR YEARS. HE'D MESSAGE REALLY YOUNG WOMEN ALL THE TIME. AND HE WAS IN A RELATIONSHIP.
1 of 10

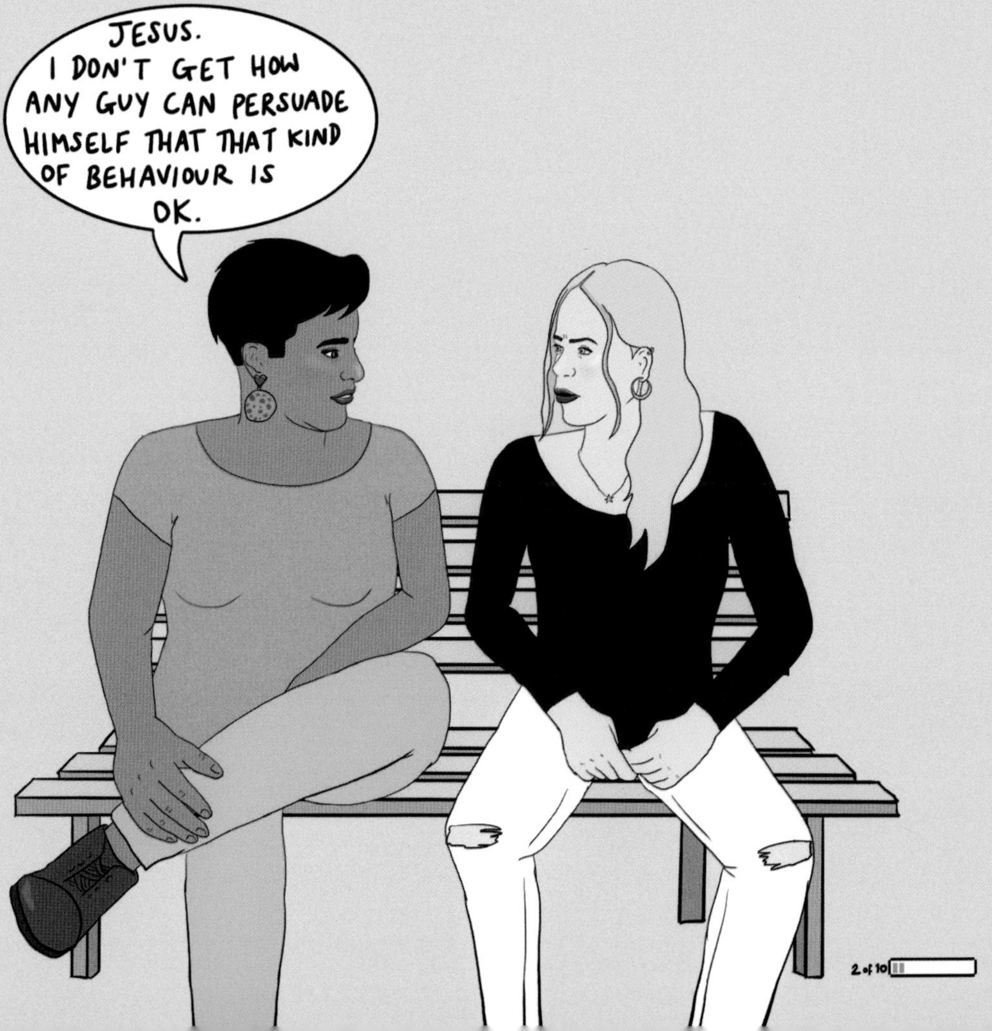
JESUS. I DON'T GET HOW ANY GUY CAN PERSUADE HIMSELF THAT THAT KIND OF BEHAVIOUR IS OK.
2 of 10

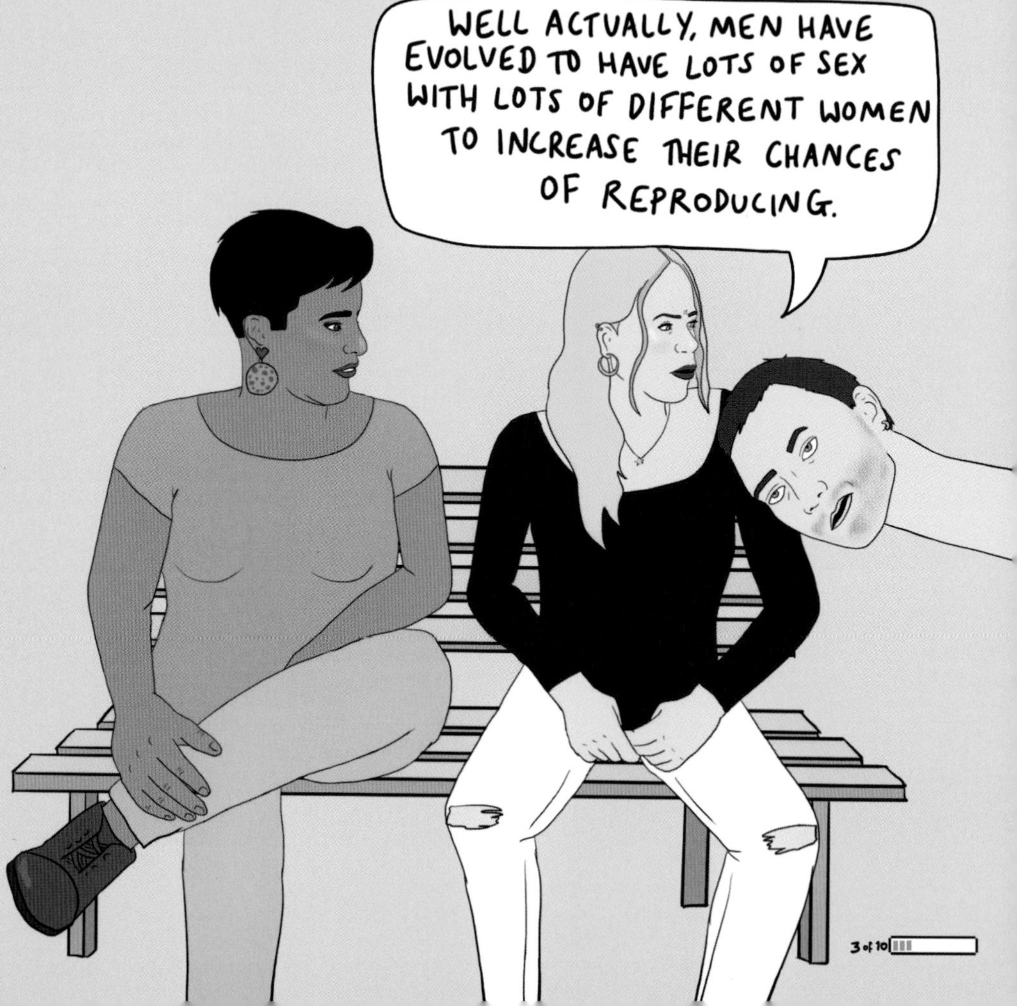
WELL ACTUALLY, MEN HAVE EVOLVED TO HAVE LOTS OF SEX WITH LOTS OF DIFFERENT WOMEN TO INCREASE THEIR CHANCES OF REPRODUCING.
3 of 10

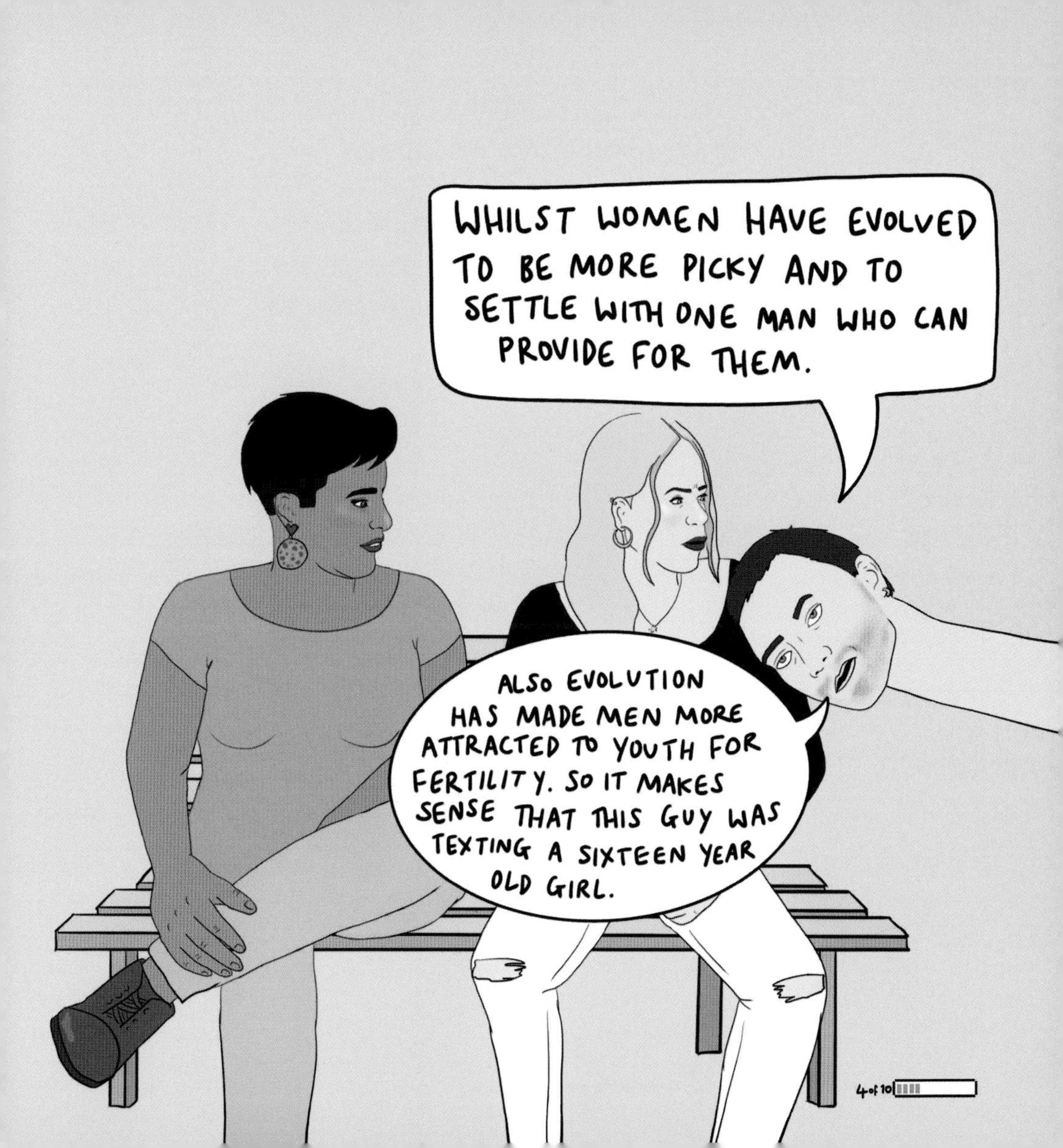
WHILST WOMEN HAVE EVOLVED TO BE MORE PICKY AND TO SETTLE WITH ONE MAN WHO CAN PROVIDE FOR THEM.
ALSO EVOLUTION HAS MADE MEN MORE ATTRACTED TO YOUTH FOR FERTILITY. SO IT MAKES SENSE THAT THIS GUY WAS TEXTING A SIXTEEN YEAR OLD GIRL.
4 of 10

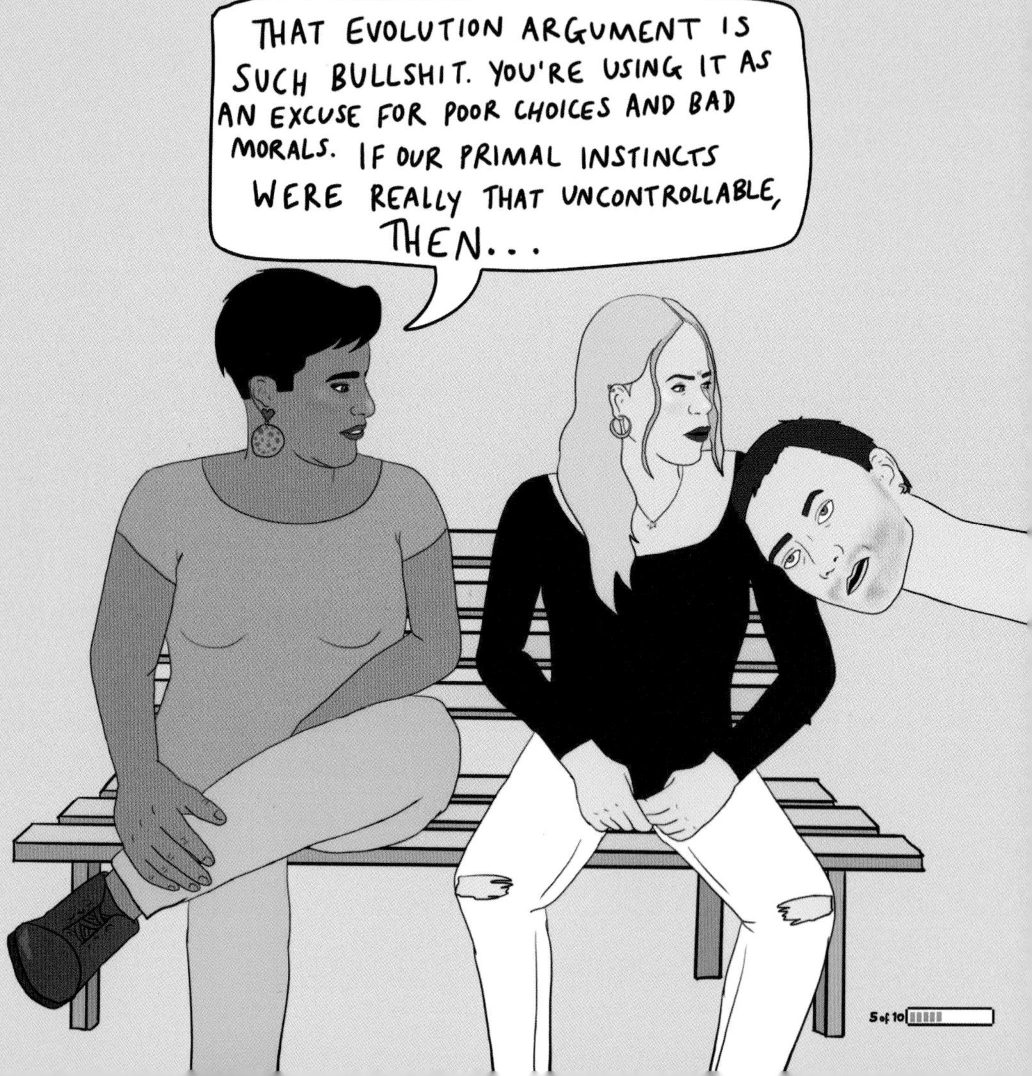
THAT EVOLUTION ARGUMENT IS SUCH BULLSHIT. YOU'RE USING IT AS AN EXCUSE FOR POOR CHOICES AND BAD MORALS. IF OUR PRIMAL INSTINCTS WERE REALLY THAT UNCONTROLLABLE, THEN...
5 of 10

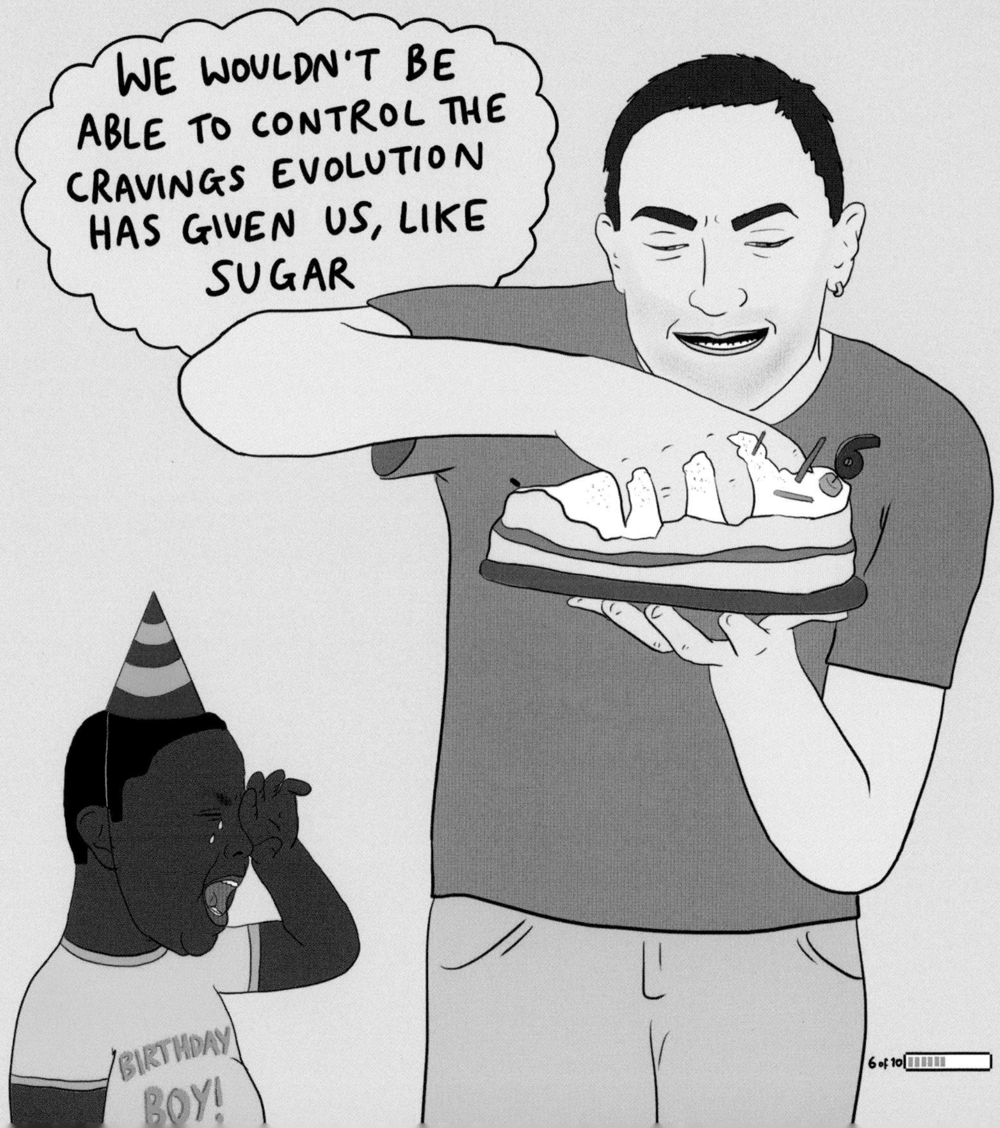
WE WOULDN'T BE ABLE TO CONTROL THE CRAVINGS EVOLUTION HAS GIVEN US, LIKE SUGAR
6
BIRTHDAY BOY!
6 of 10

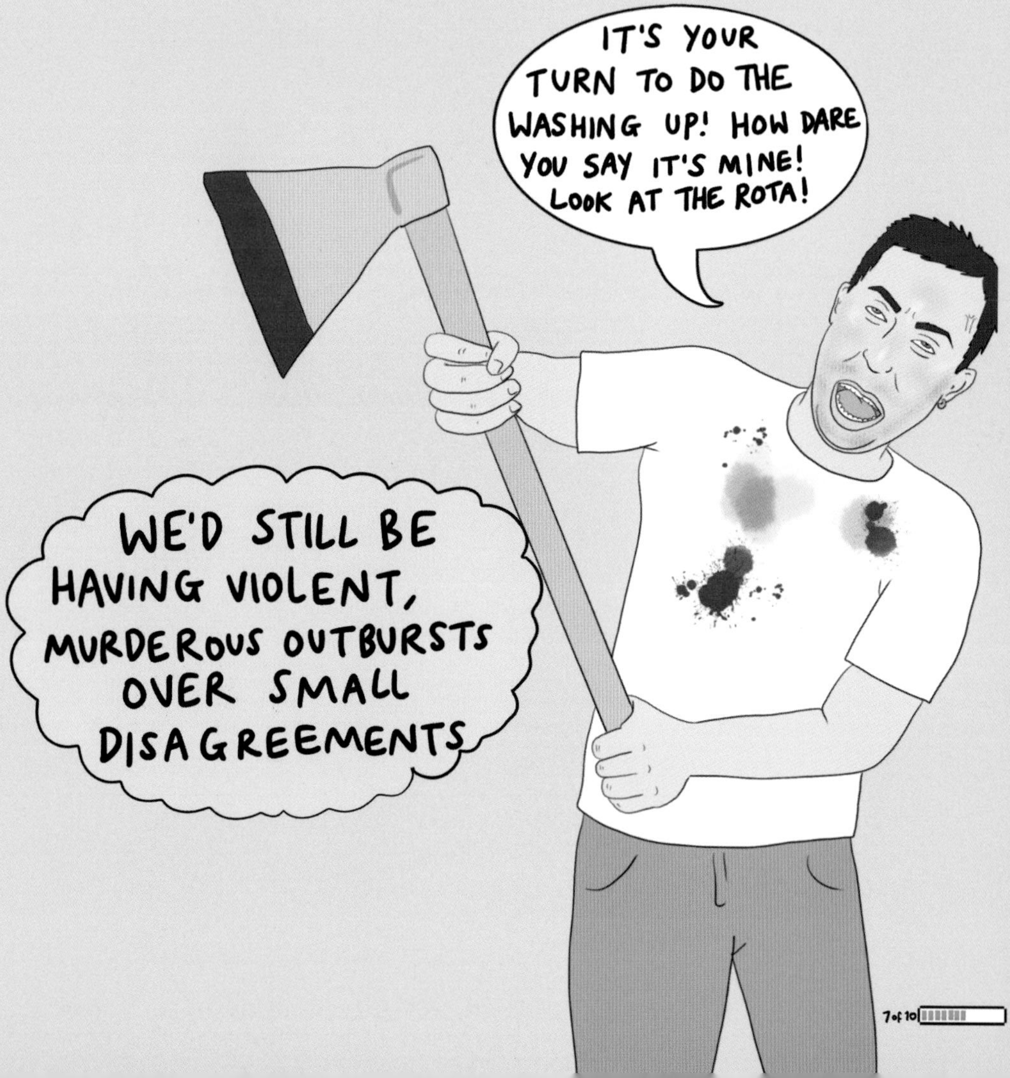
IT'S YOUR TURN TO DO THE WASHING UP! HOW DARE YOU SAY IT'S MINE! LOOK AT THE ROTA!
WE'D STILL BE HAVING VIOLENT, MURDEROUS OUTBURSTS OVER SMALL DISAGREEMENTS

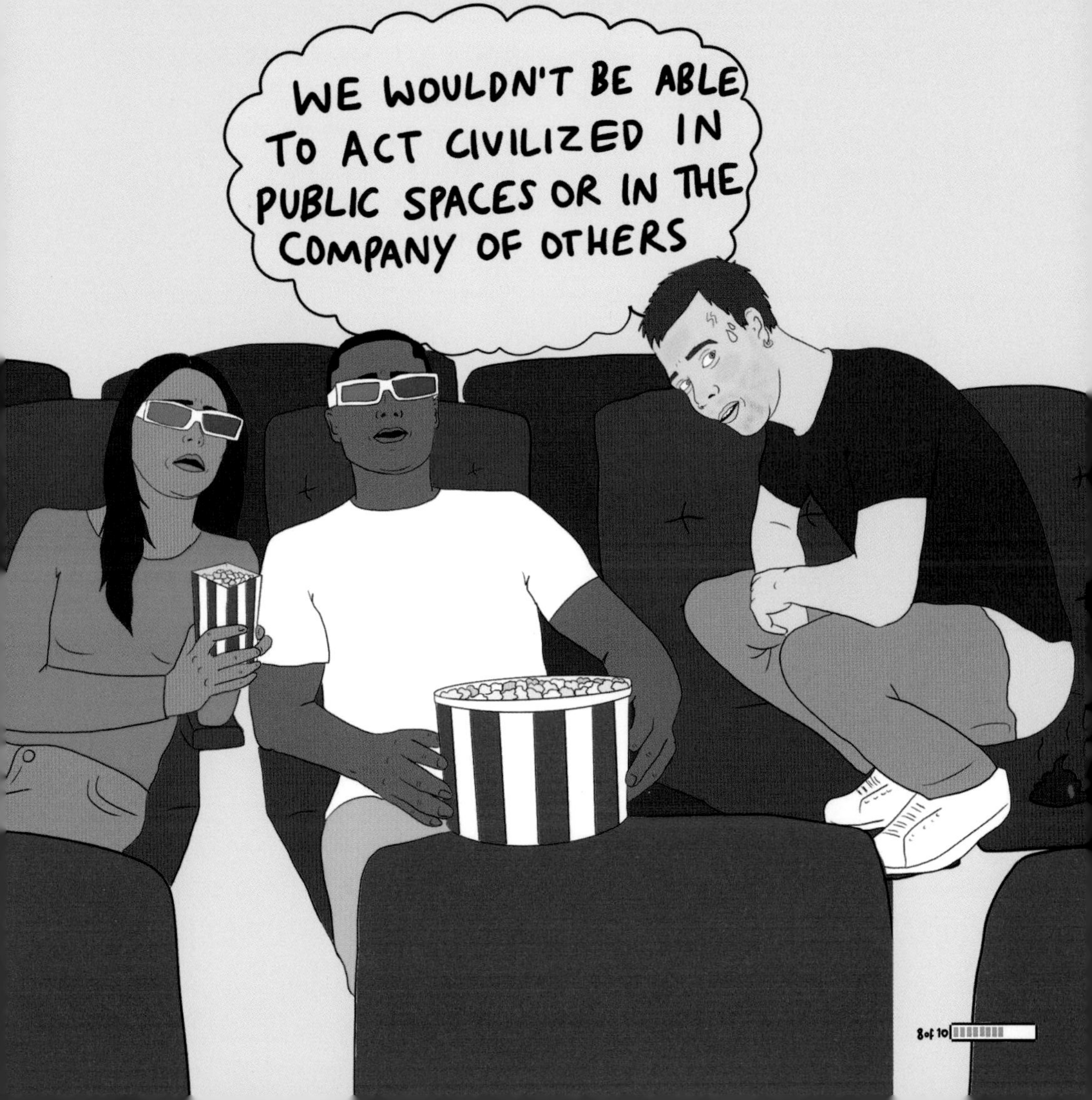
WE WOULDN'T BE ABLE TO ACT CIVILIZED IN PUBLIC SPACES OR IN THE COMPANY OF OTHERS
8 of 10

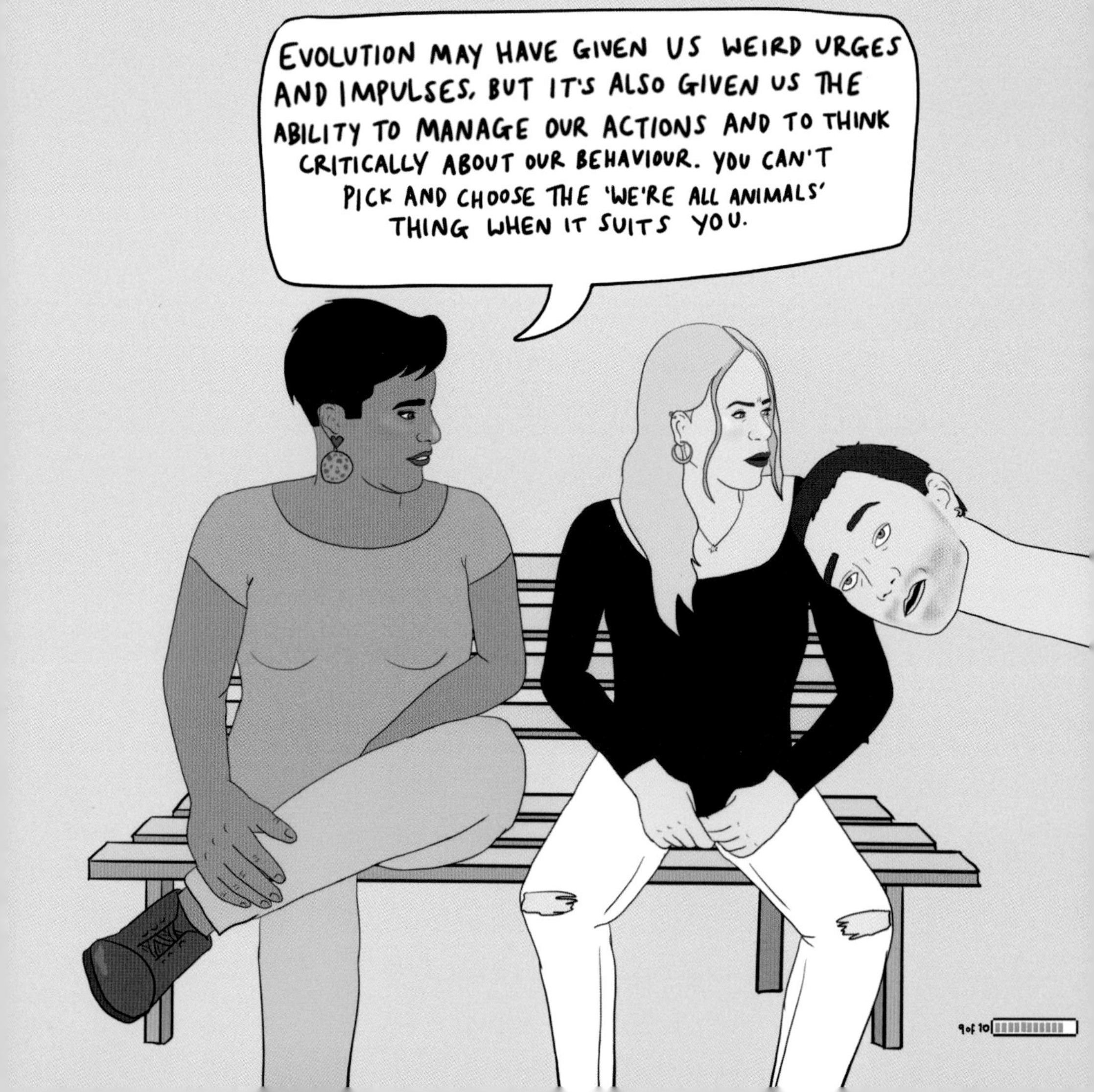
EVOLUTION MAY HAVE GIVEN US WEIRD URGES AND IMPULSES, BUT IT'S ALSO GIVEN US THE ABILITY TO MANAGE OUR ACTIONS AND TO THINK CRITICALLY ABOUT OUR BEHAVIOUR. YOU CAN'T PICK AND CHOOSE THE 'WE'RE ALL ANIMALS' THING WHEN IT SUITS YOU.
9of 10

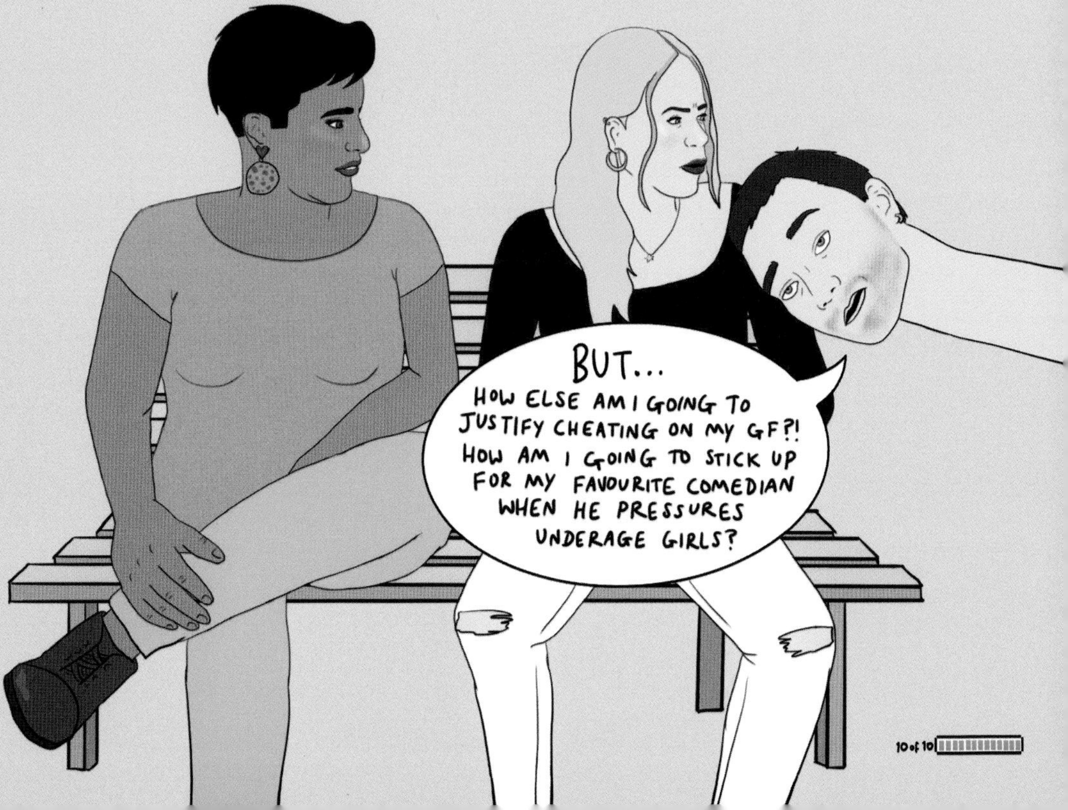
BUT...
HOW ELSE AM I GOING TO JUSTIFY CHEATING ON MY GF?! HOW AM I GOING TO STICK UP FOR MY FAVOURITE COMEDIAN WHEN HE PRESSURES UNDERAGE GIRLS?
10 of 10

HOW TO GET A GUY TO BE PASSIONATE ABOUT SEXISM

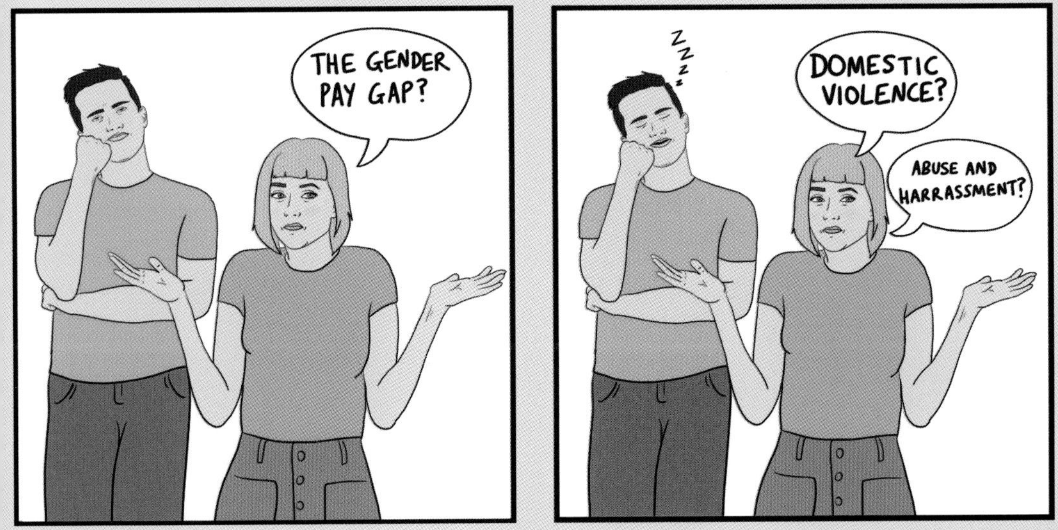
THE GENDER PAY GAP?
DOMESTIC VIOLENCE?
ABUSE AND HARRASSMENT?
ZZZ

1 of 2

I ONLY DATE MEN WHO ARE 6 FEET OR TALLER
WTF?!!
THAT IS SO SEXIST TOWARDS MEN!
WOMEN ARE SUCH HYPOCRITES!

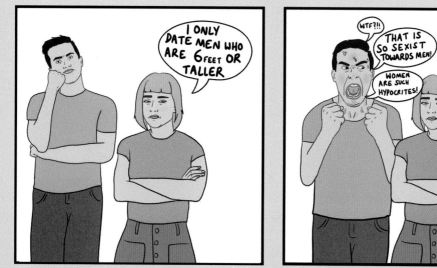

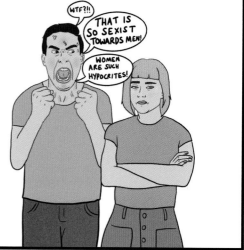

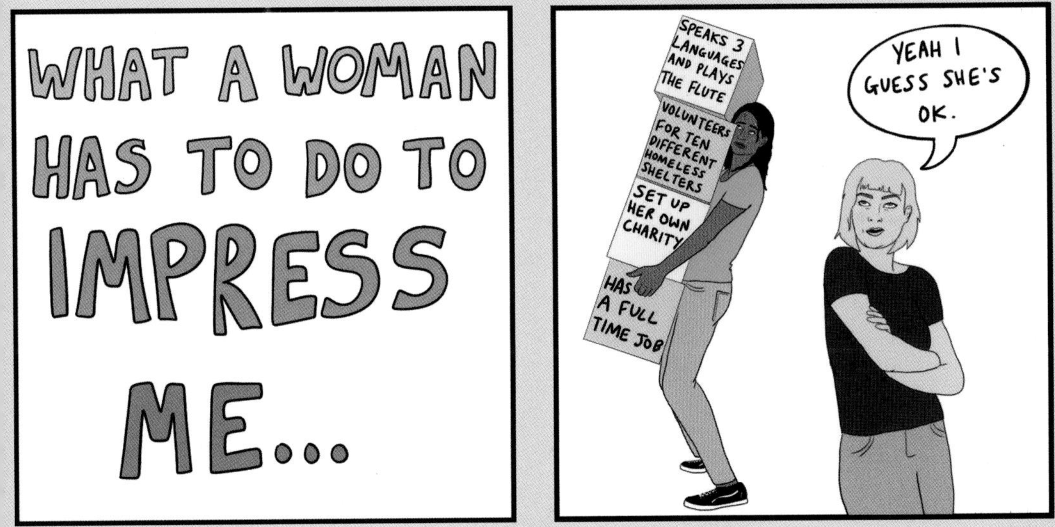
WHAT A WOMAN HAS TO DO TO IMPRESS ME...
SPEAKS 3 LANGUAGES AND PLAYS THE FLUTE
VOLUNTEERS FOR TEN DIFFERENT HOMELESS SHELTERS
SET UP HER OWN CHARITY
HAS A FULL TIME JOB
YEAH I GUESS SHE'S OK.

1 of 2

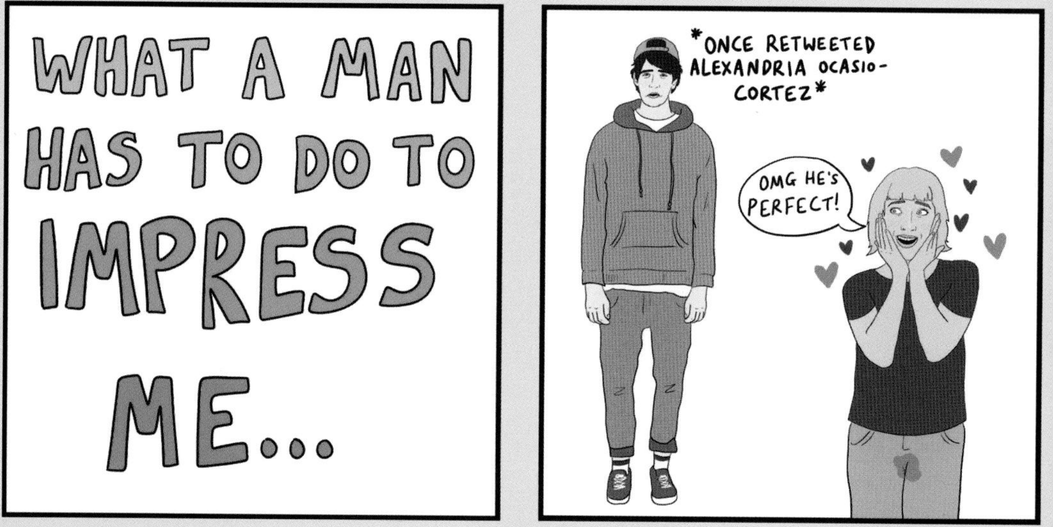
WHAT A MAN HAS TO DO TO IMPRESS ME...
ONCE RETWEETED ALEXANDRIA OCASIO-CORTEZ
OMG HE'S PERFECT!

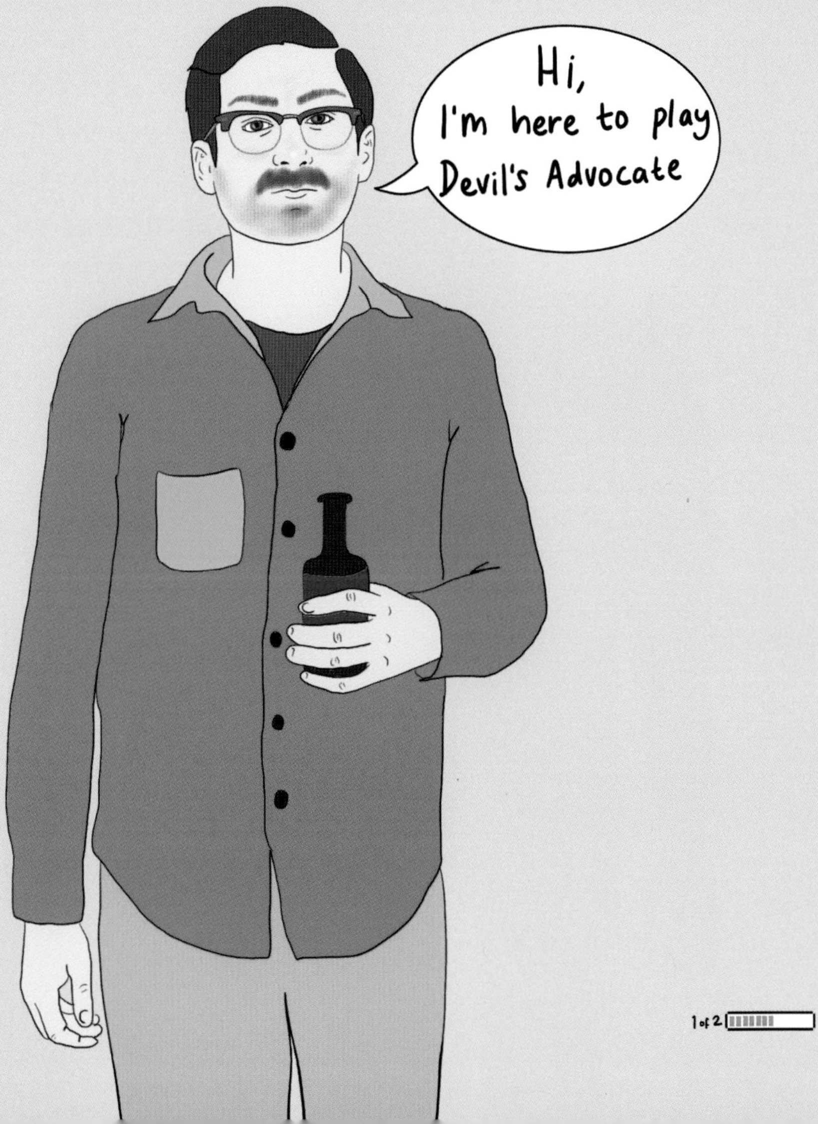
Hi,
I'm here to play
Devil's Advocate
1 of 2

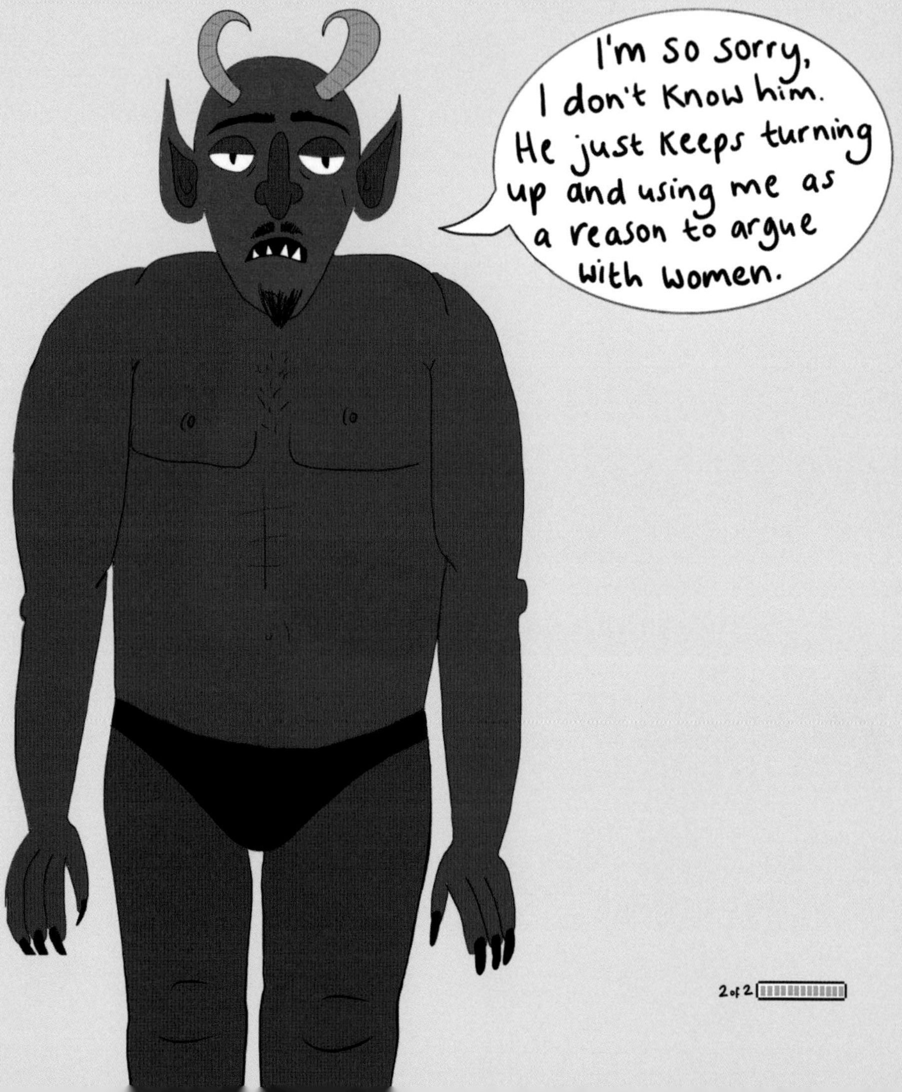
I'm so sorry, I don't know him. He just keeps turning up and using me as a reason to argue with women.
2 of 2

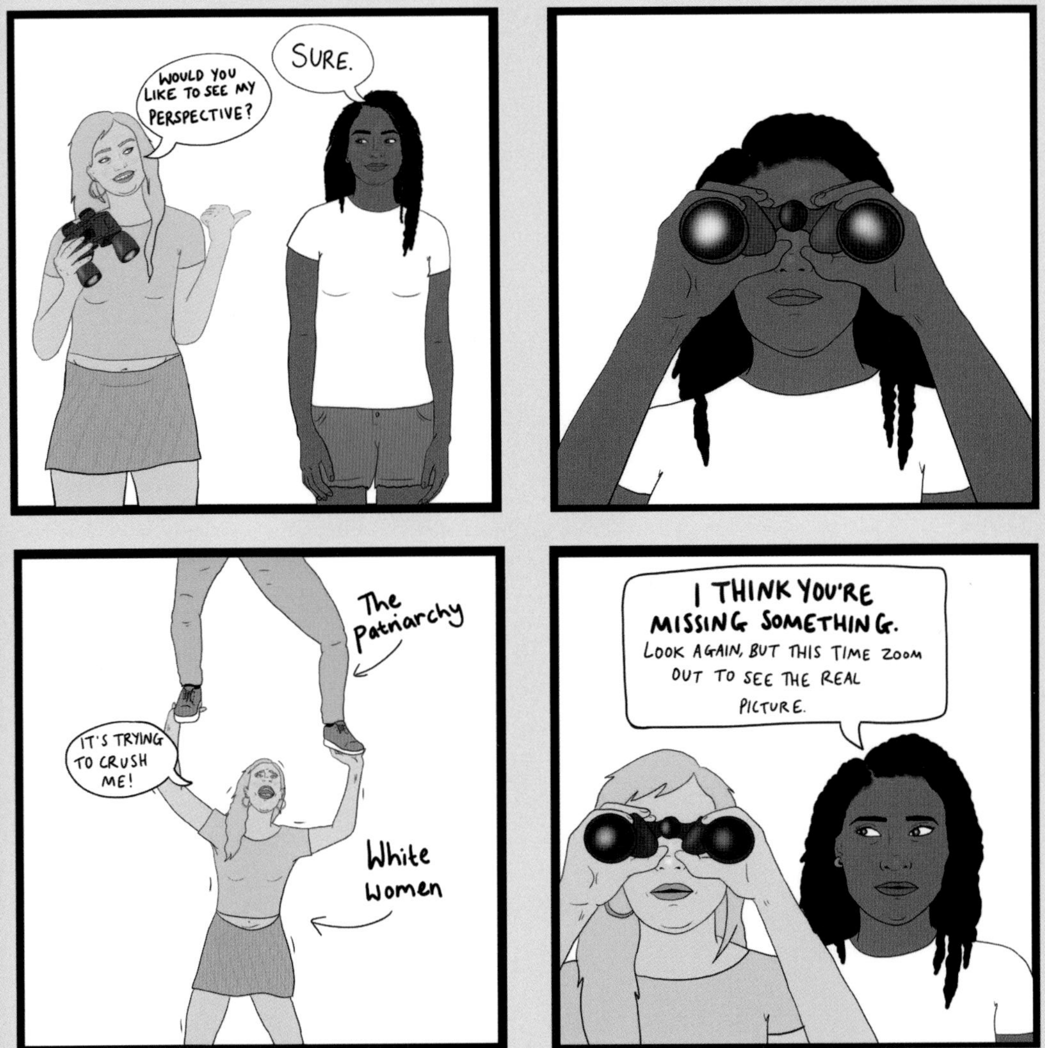
WOULD YOU LIKE TO SEE MY PERSPECTIVE?
SURE.
The Patriarchy
IT'S TRYING TO CRUSH ME!
White Women
I THINK YOU'RE MISSING SOMETHING.
LOOK AGAIN, BUT THIS TIME ZOOM OUT TO SEE THE REAL PICTURE.

1 of 2

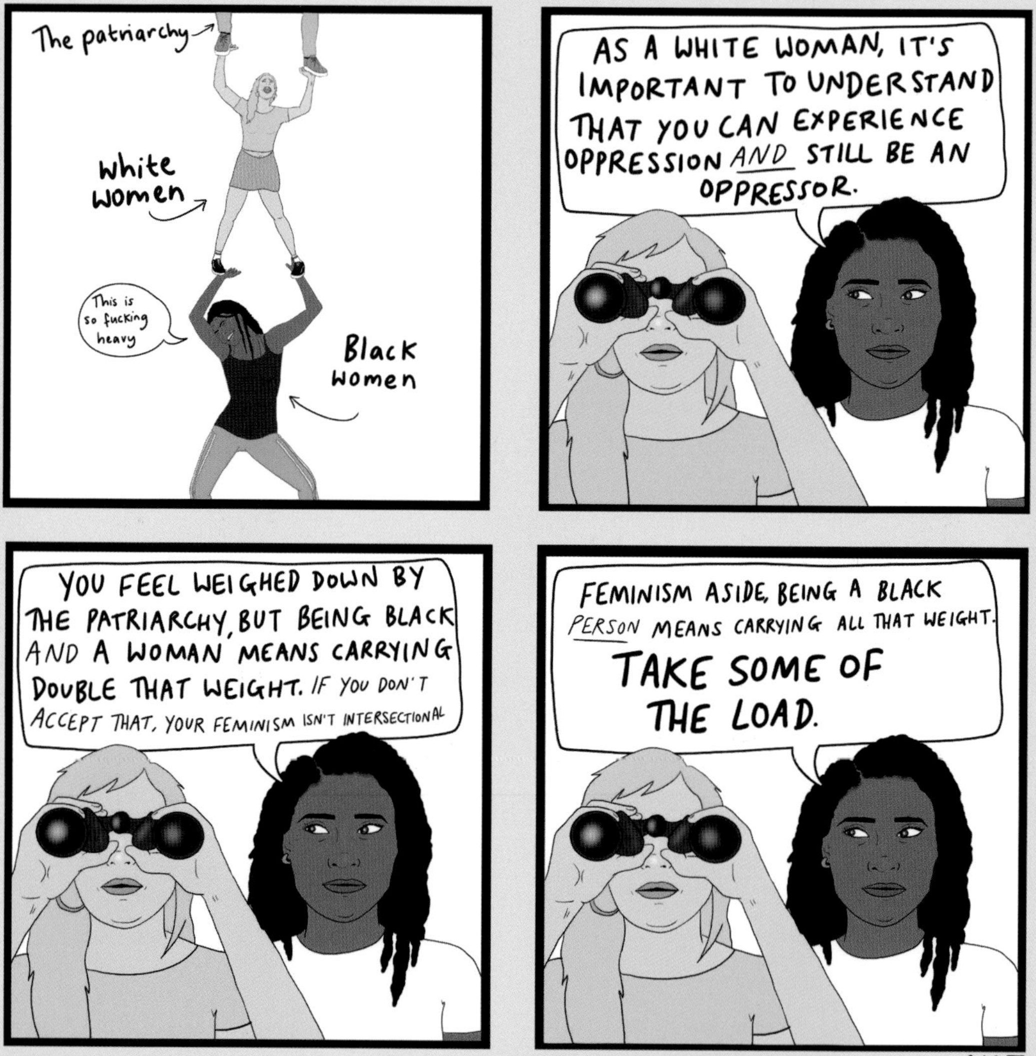
The patriarchy
white women
This is so fucking heavy
Black women
AS A WHITE WOMAN, IT'S IMPORTANT TO UNDERSTAND THAT YOU CAN EXPERIENCE OPPRESSION AND STILL BE AN OPPRESSOR.
YOU FEEL WEIGHED DOWN BY THE PATRIARCHY, BUT BEING BLACK AND A WOMAN MEANS CARRYING DOUBLE THAT WEIGHT. IF YOU DON'T ACCEPT THAT, YOUR FEMINISM ISN'T INTERSECTIONAL
FEMINISM ASIDE, BEING A BLACK PERSON MEANS CARRYING ALL THAT WEIGHT.
TAKE SOME OF THE LOAD.

2 of 2

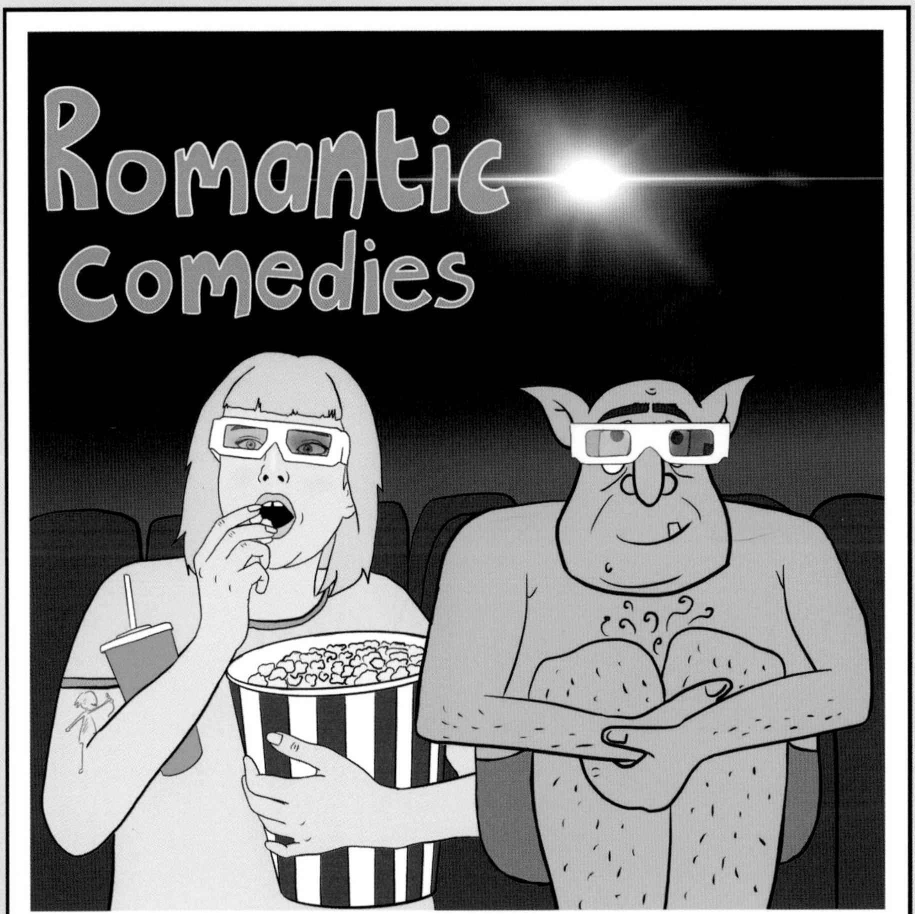
Romantic
Comedies

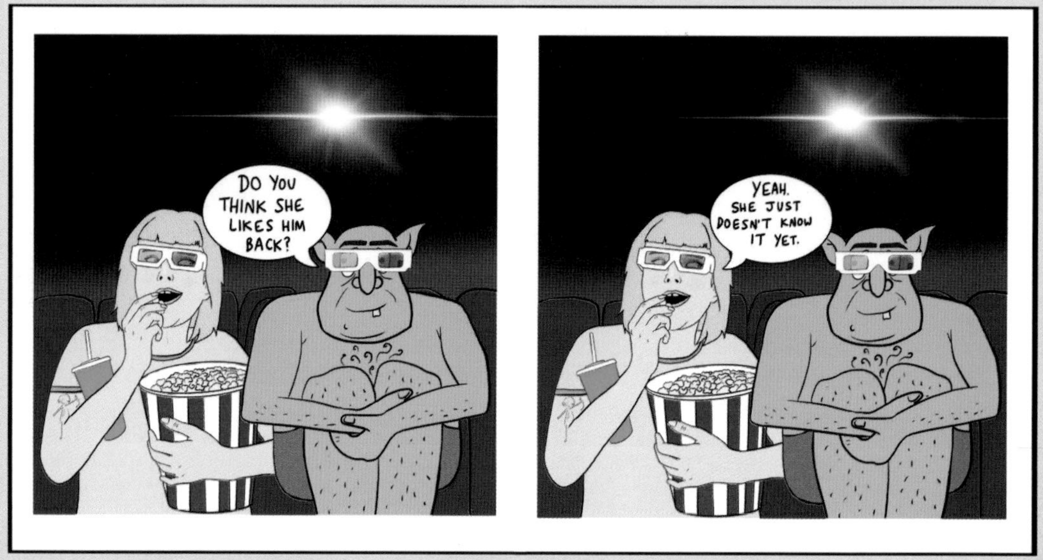
DO YOU THINK SHE LIKES HIM BACK?
YEAH. SHE JUST DOESN'T KNOW IT YET.

The 4 types
of female lead
in a
Romantic Comedy

Career boss bitch

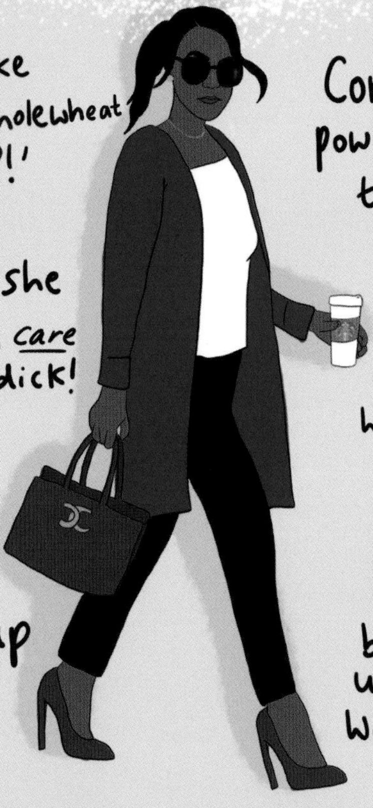

Says stuff like 'Where's my wholewheat bagel?!'

Acts like she doesn't even care about your dick!

Lighten up honey!

Confident and powerful - say goodbye to your boner!

Scary!! Men scream when they see her!

Has a great job but is secretly so unhappy - all she wants is a man!

1 of 4

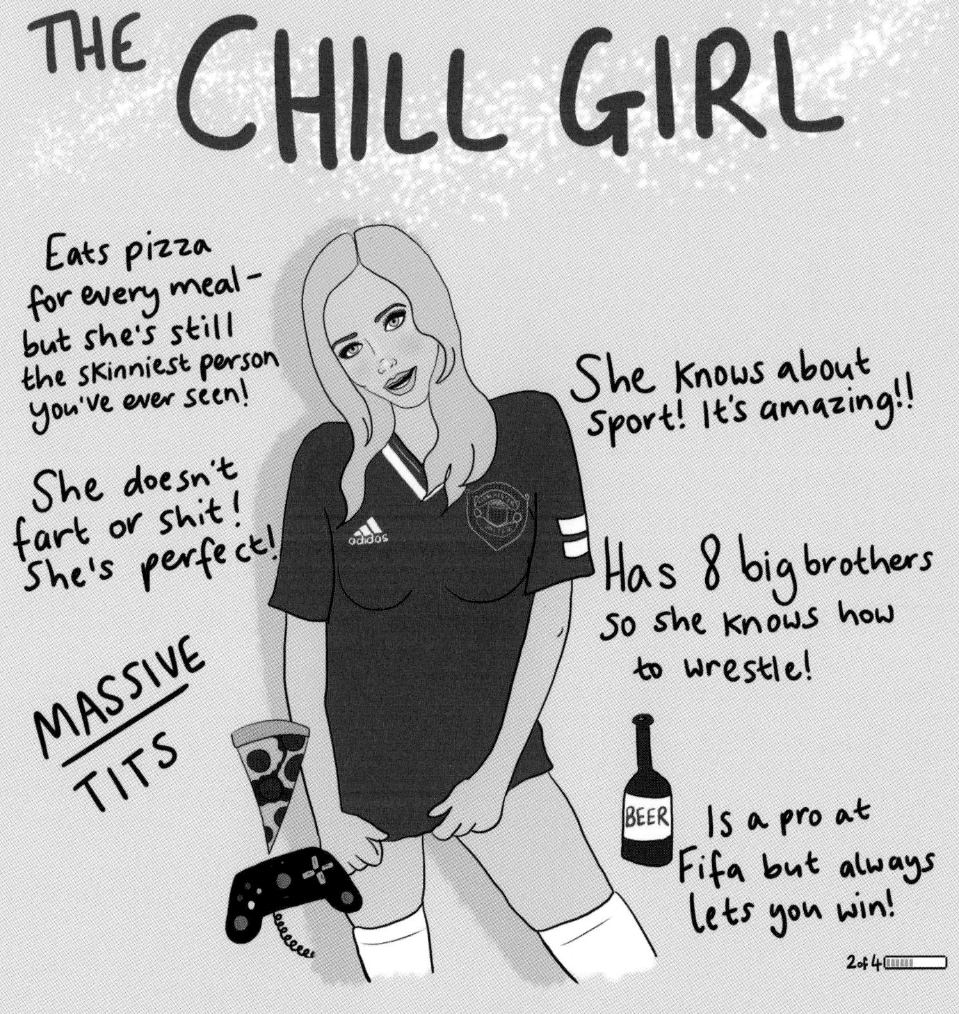
THE CHILL GIRL
Eats pizza for every meal- but she's still the skinniest person you've ever seen!
She knows about sport! It's amazing!!
She doesn't fart or shit! She's perfect!
adidas
Has 8 big brothers so she knows how to wrestle!
MASSIVE TITS
BEER
Is a pro at Fifa but always lets you win!
2of4

MOODY SMART BITCH

Has aspirations to be a lawyer or doctor and not a wife!!!

Can be found sitting under a tree reading a book and calling you an idiot even though she's secretly in love with you!

Too many opinions! Shoosh!!

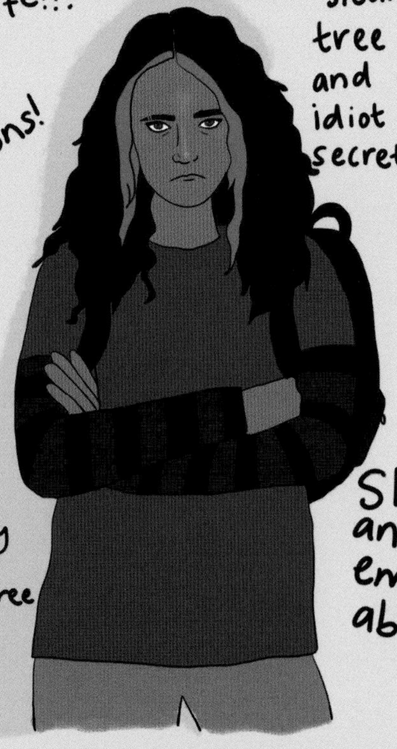

Smart! (Yuck!)

She'll suddenly become hot and popular so you agree to date her!

She's a feminist and isn't even embarrassed about it!!!

3 of 4

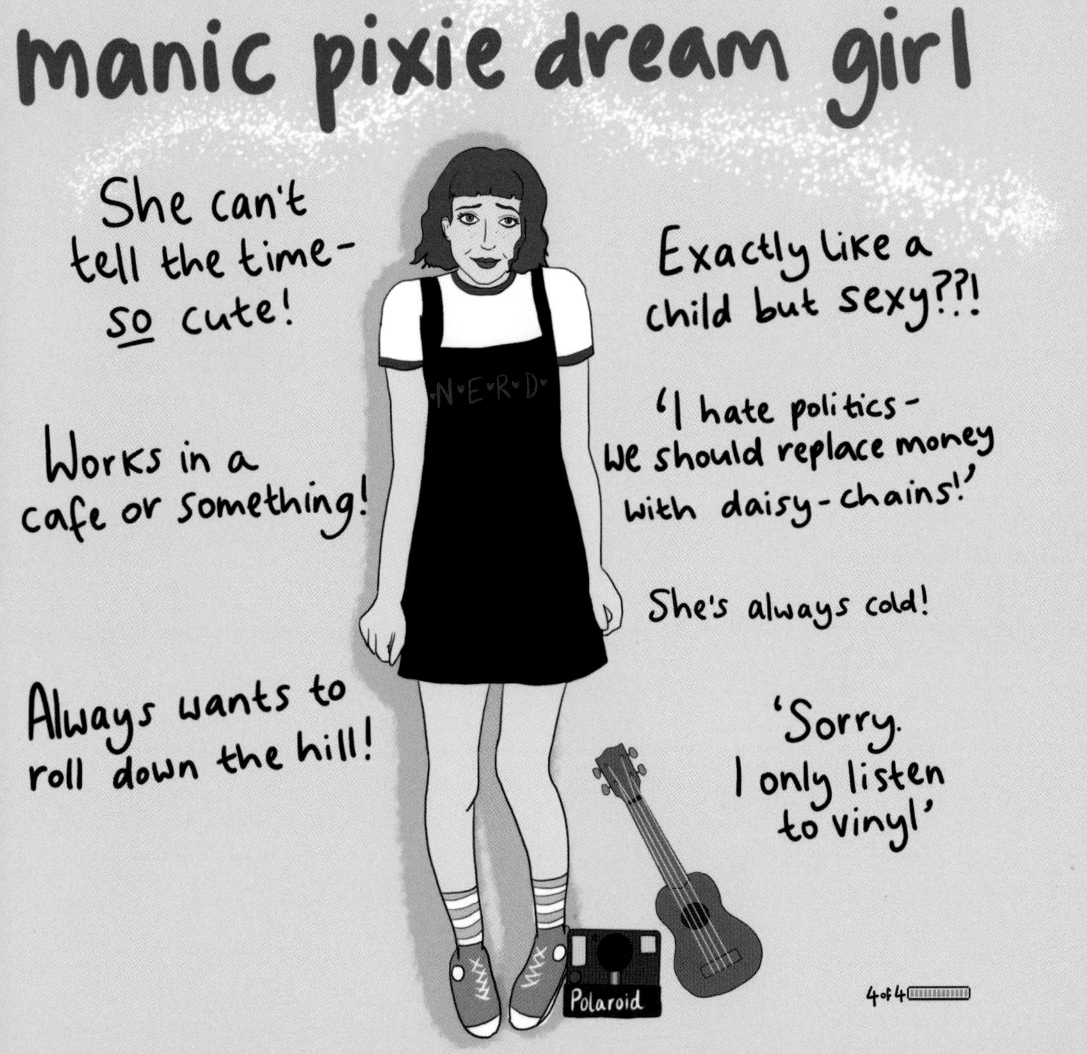
manic pixie dream girl
She can't tell the time - so cute!
Exactly like a child but sexy??!
N•E•R•D
Works in a cafe or something!
'I hate politics - we should replace money with daisy-chains!'
She's always cold!
Always wants to roll down the hill!
'Sorry. I only listen to vinyl'
Polaroid
4 of 4

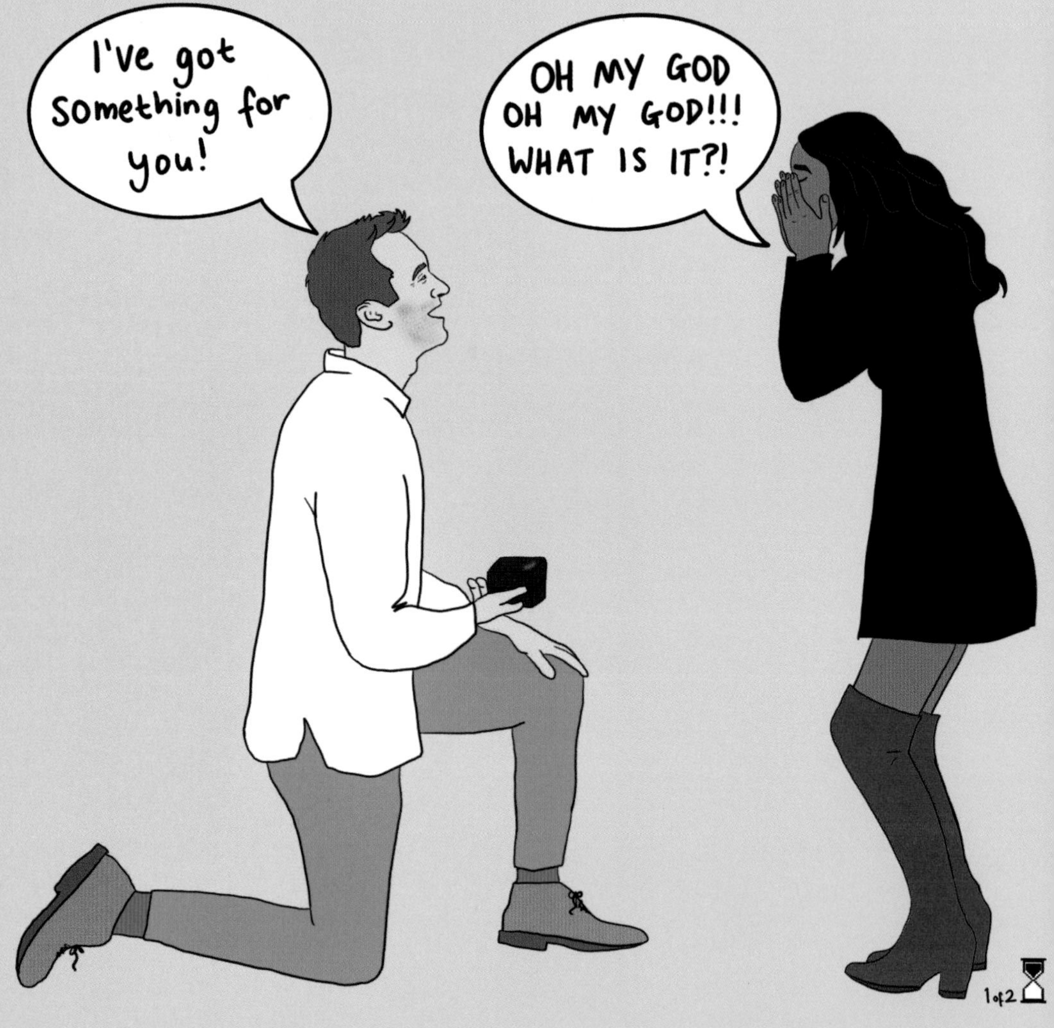
I've got something for you!
OH MY GOD OH MY GOD!!! WHAT IS IT?!
1 of 2

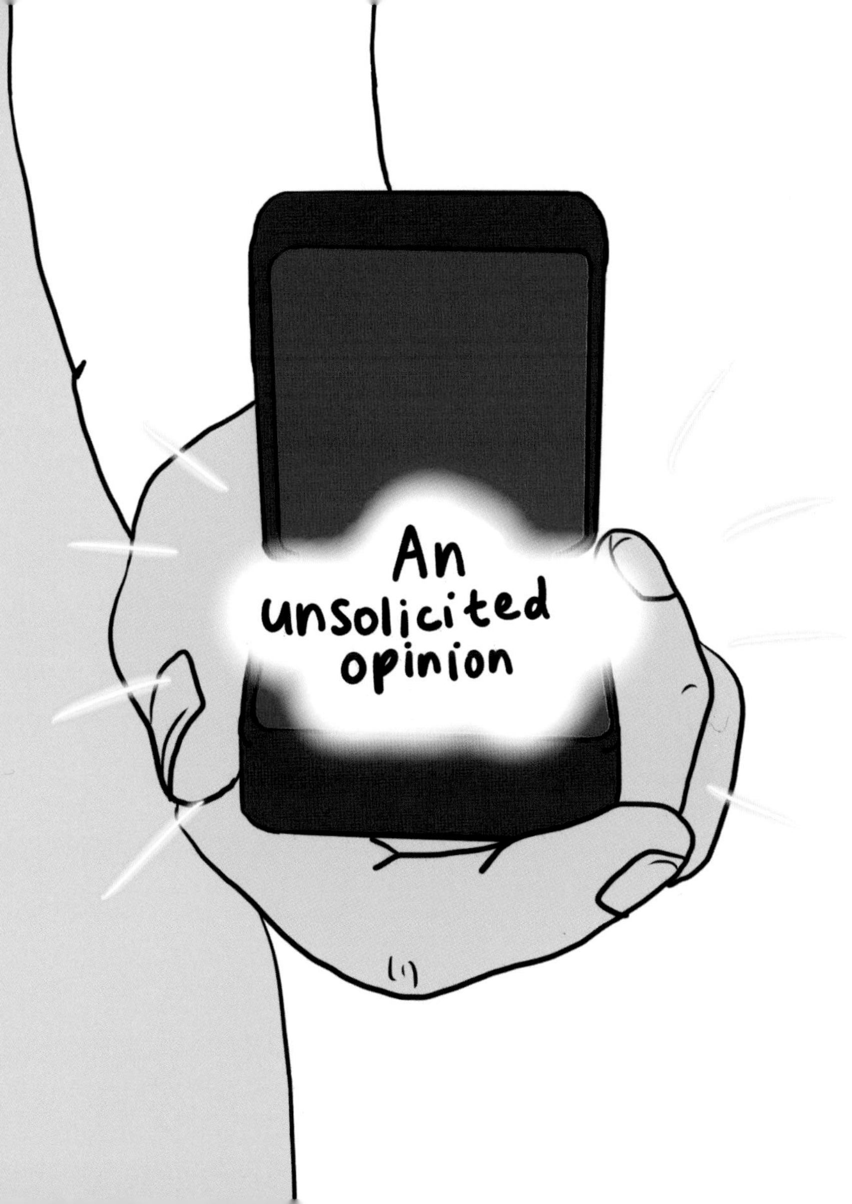
An
unsolicited
opinion

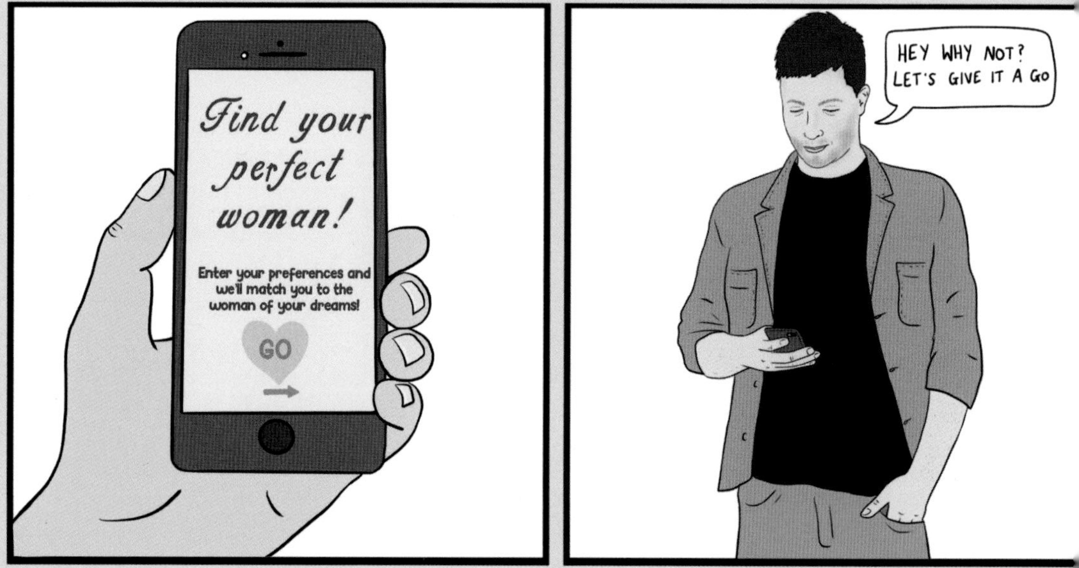
Find your perfect woman!
Enter your preferences and we'll match you to the woman of your dreams!
GO
HEY WHY NOT? LET'S GIVE IT A GO

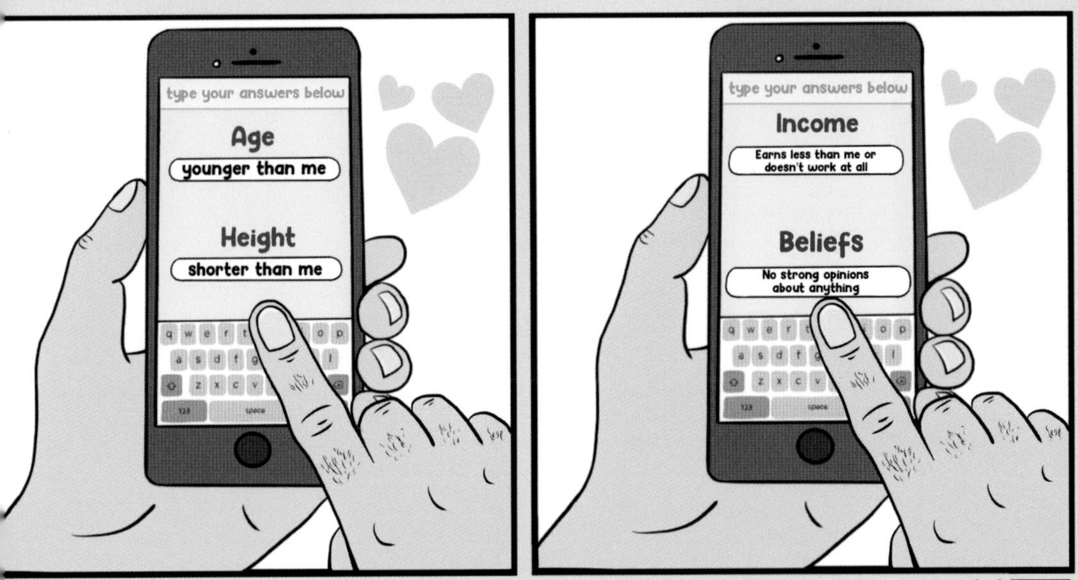
type your answers below
Age
younger than me
Height
shorter than me
type your answers below
Income
Earns less than me or doesn't work at all
Beliefs
No strong opinions about anything

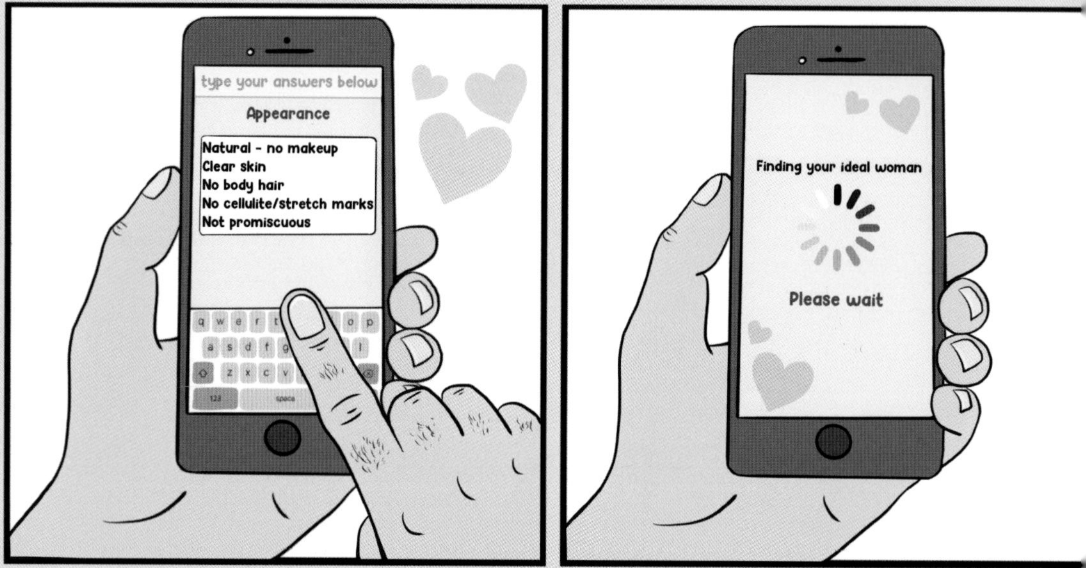
type your answers below
Appearance
Natural - no makeup
Clear skin
No body hair
No cellulite/stretch marks
Not promiscuous
Finding your ideal woman
Please wait

3 of 4

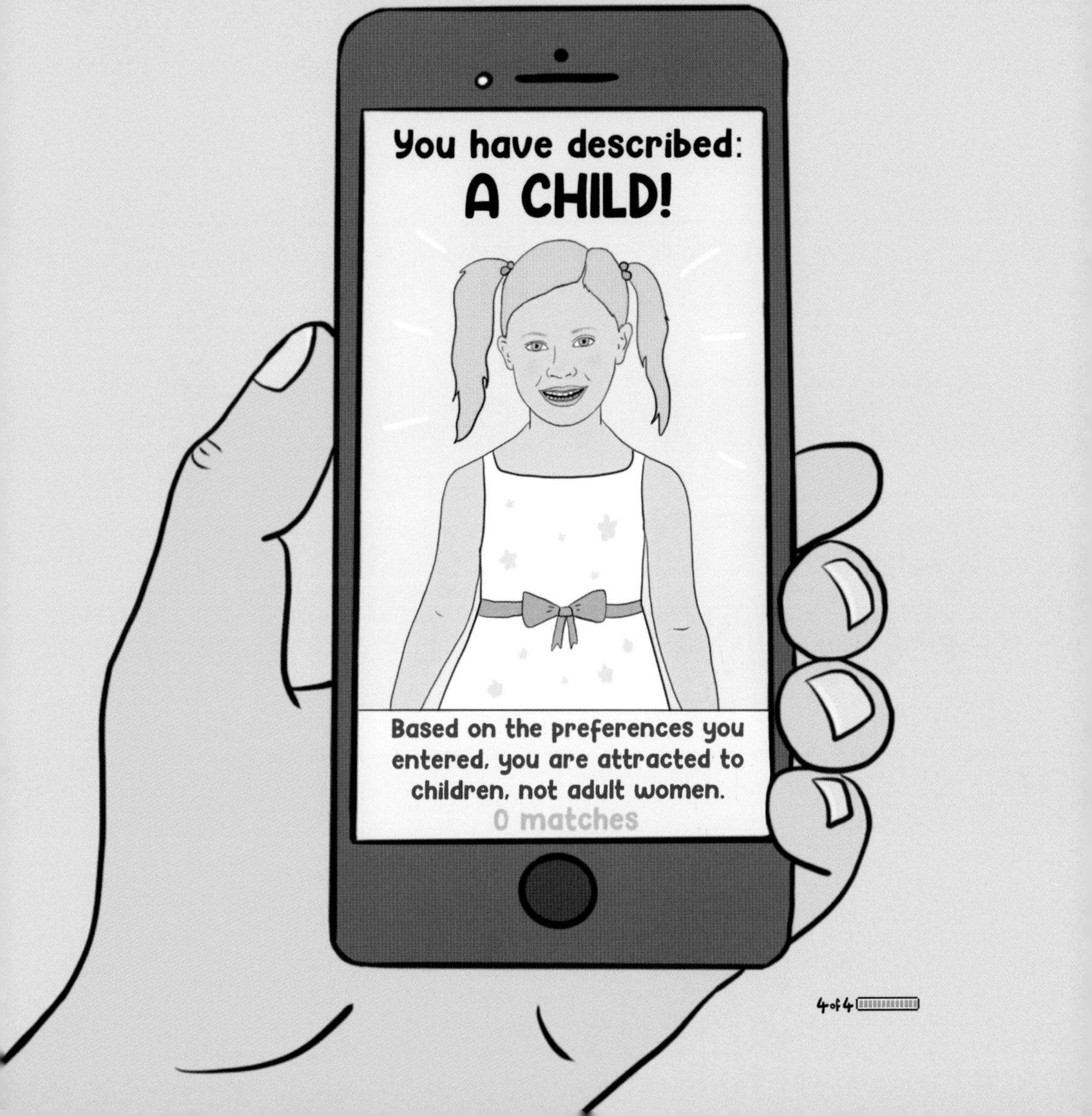
You have described:
A CHILD!
Based on the preferences you entered, you are attracted to children, not adult women.
0 matches
4 of 4

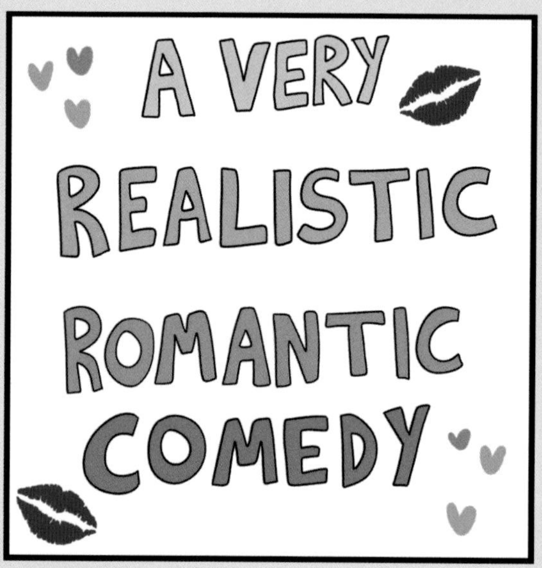
A VERY
REALISTIC
ROMANTIC
COMEDY

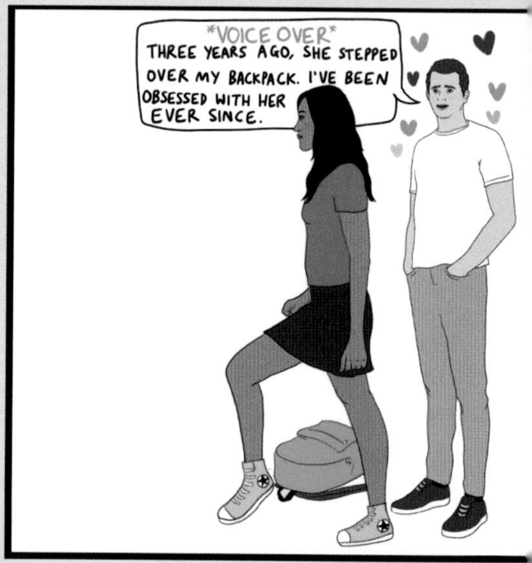
VOICE OVER
THREE YEARS AGO, SHE STEPPED OVER MY BACKPACK. I'VE BEEN OBSESSED WITH HER EVER SINCE.

1 of 5

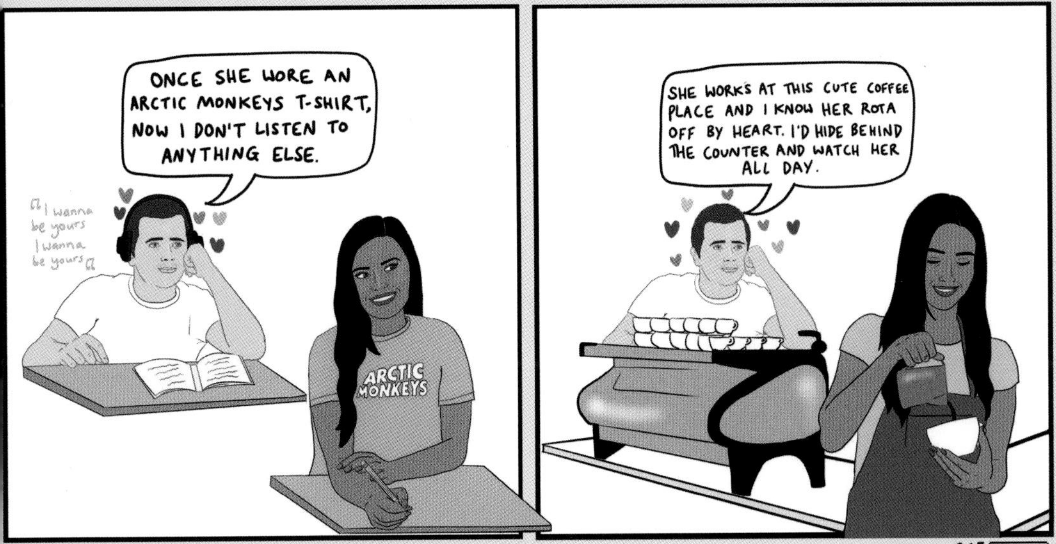
ONCE SHE WORE AN ARCTIC MONKEYS T-SHIRT, NOW I DON'T LISTEN TO ANYTHING ELSE.
"I wanna be yours I wanna be yours"
ARCTIC MONKEYS
SHE WORKS AT THIS CUTE COFFEE PLACE AND I KNOW HER ROTA OFF BY HEART. I'D HIDE BEHIND THE COUNTER AND WATCH HER ALL DAY.

2 of 5

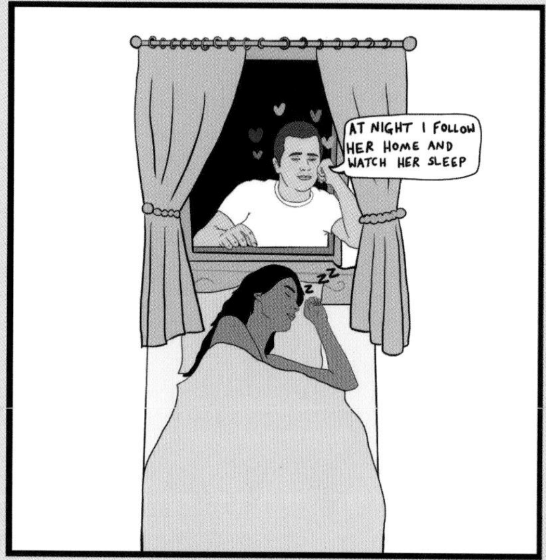
AT NIGHT I FOLLOW HER HOME AND WATCH HER SLEEP
Z Z Z

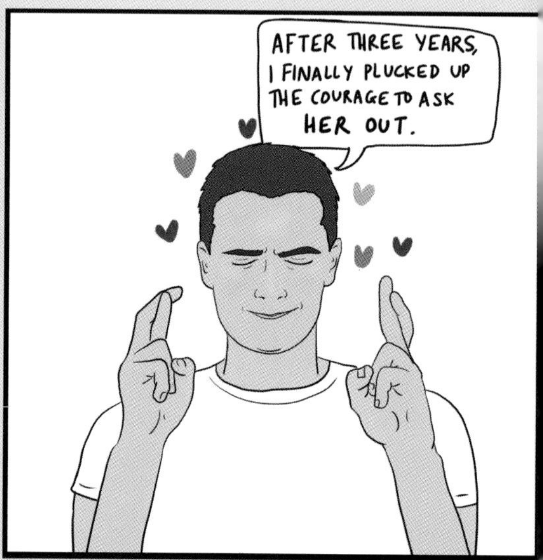
AFTER THREE YEARS, I FINALLY PLUCKED UP THE COURAGE TO ASK HER OUT.

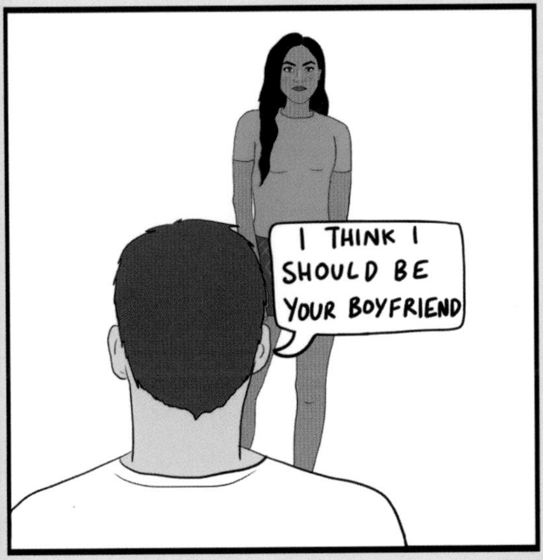
I THINK I SHOULD BE YOUR BOYFRIEND

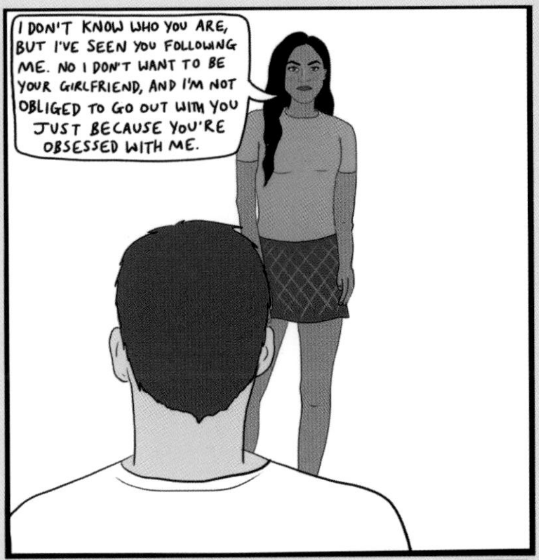
I DON'T KNOW WHO YOU ARE, BUT I'VE SEEN YOU FOLLOWING ME. NO I DON'T WANT TO BE YOUR GIRLFRIEND, AND I'M NOT OBLIGED TO GO OUT WITH YOU JUST BECAUSE YOU'RE OBSESSED WITH ME.

4 of 5

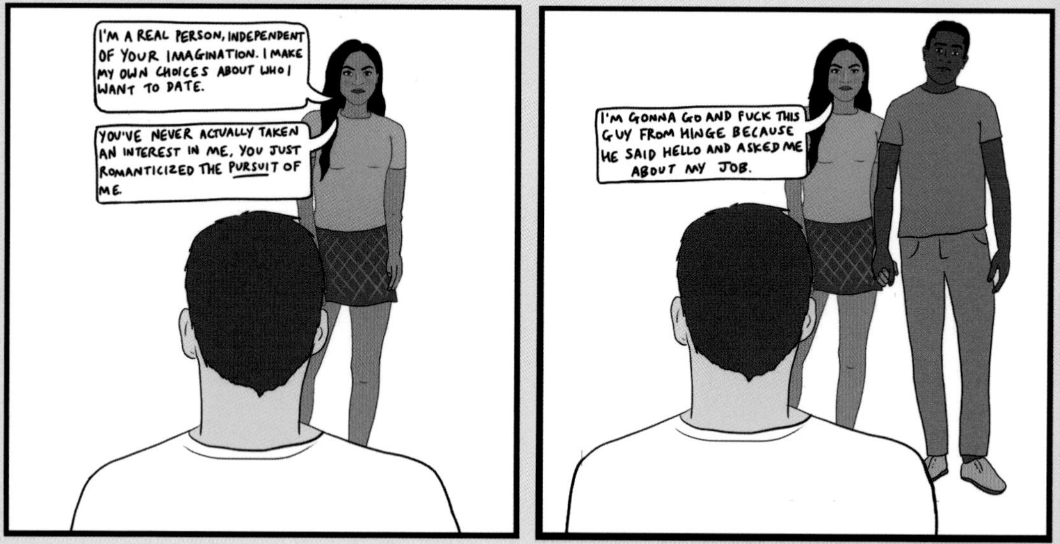
I'M A REAL PERSON, INDEPENDENT OF YOUR IMAGINATION. I MAKE MY OWN CHOICES ABOUT WHO I WANT TO DATE.
YOU'VE NEVER ACTUALLY TAKEN AN INTEREST IN ME, YOU JUST ROMANTICIZED THE PURSUIT OF ME.
I'M GONNA GO AND FUCK THIS GUY FROM HINGE BECAUSE HE SAID HELLO AND ASKED ME ABOUT MY JOB.

5 of 5

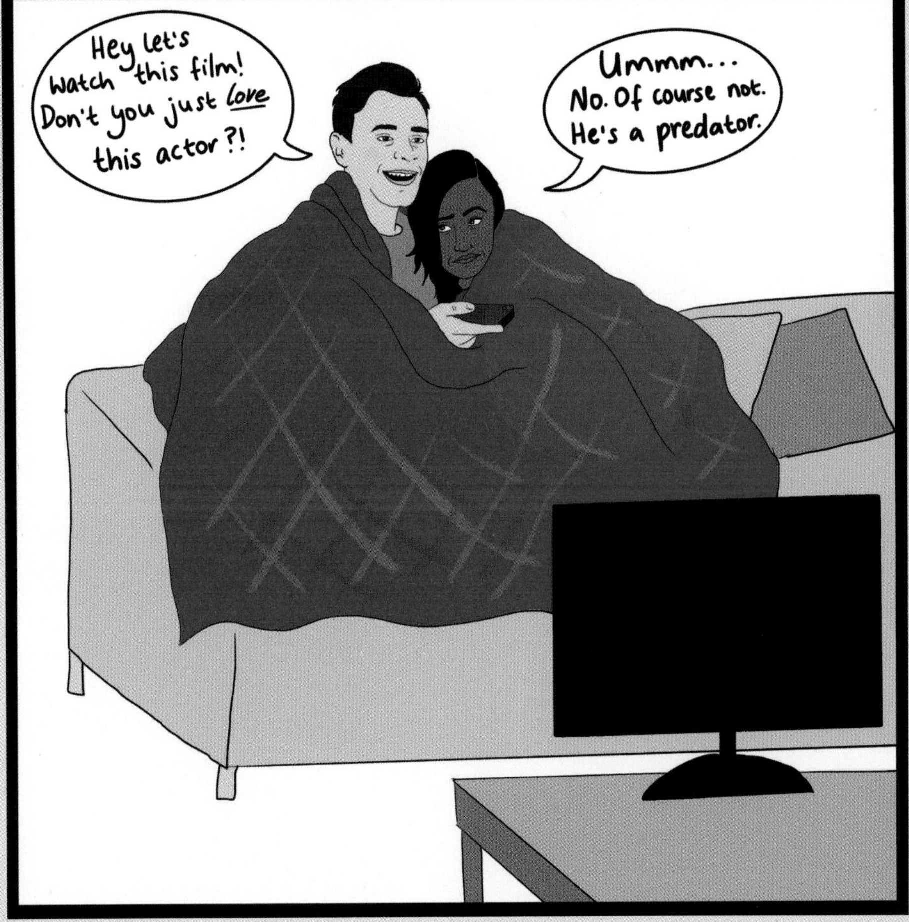
Hey let's watch this film! Don't you just love this actor?!
Ummm... No. Of course not. He's a predator.

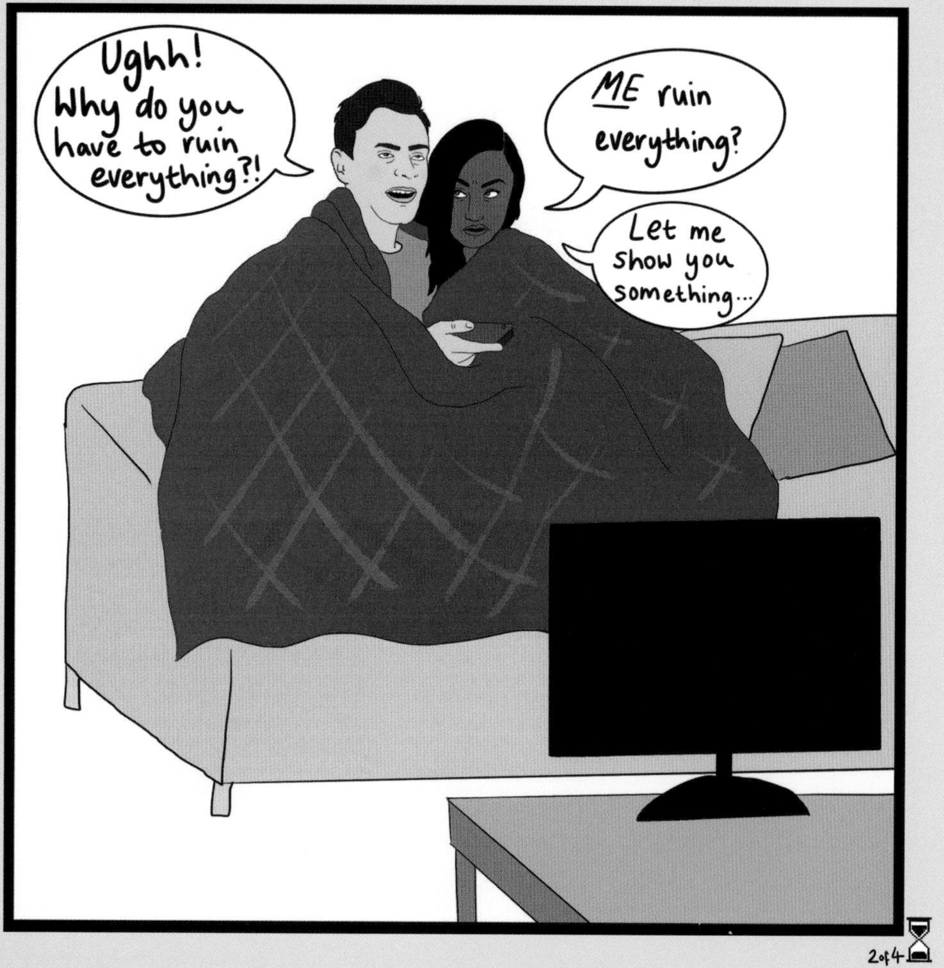
Ughh! Why do you have to ruin everything?!
ME ruin everything?
Let me show you something...
2 of 4

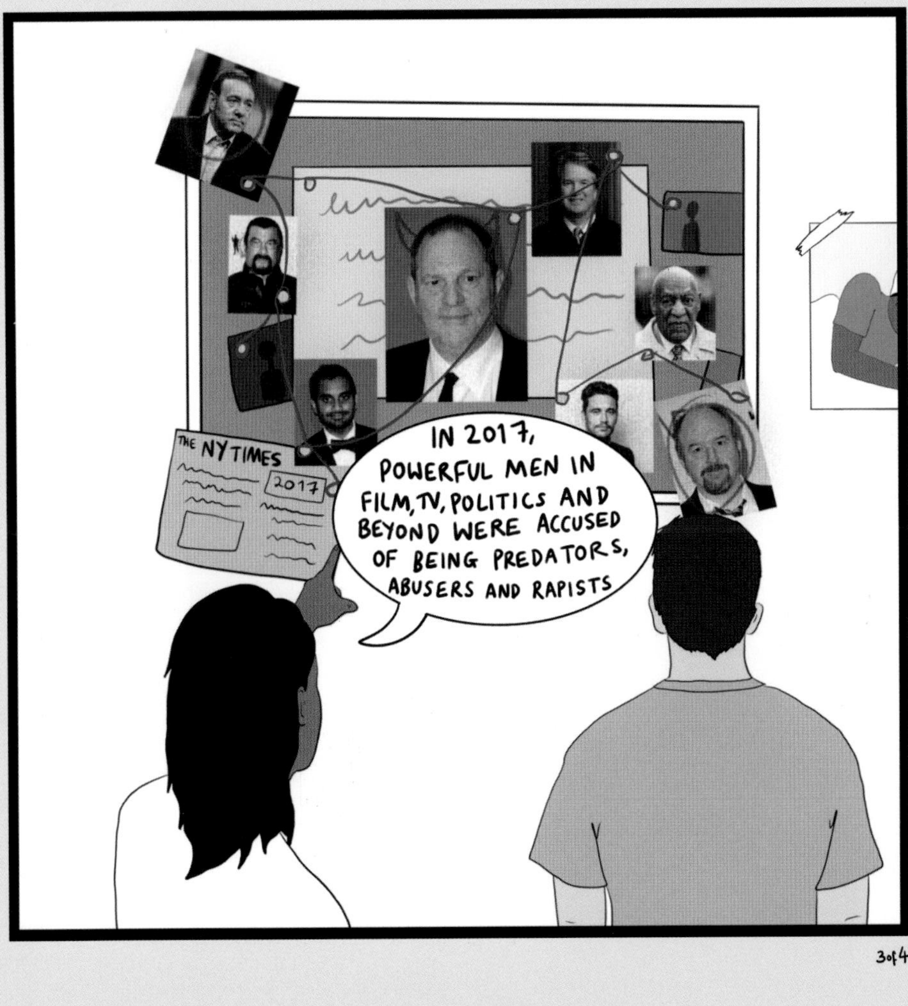
THE NY TIMES
2017
IN 2017, POWERFUL MEN IN FILM, TV, POLITICS AND BEYOND WERE ACCUSED OF BEING PREDATORS, ABUSERS AND RAPISTS

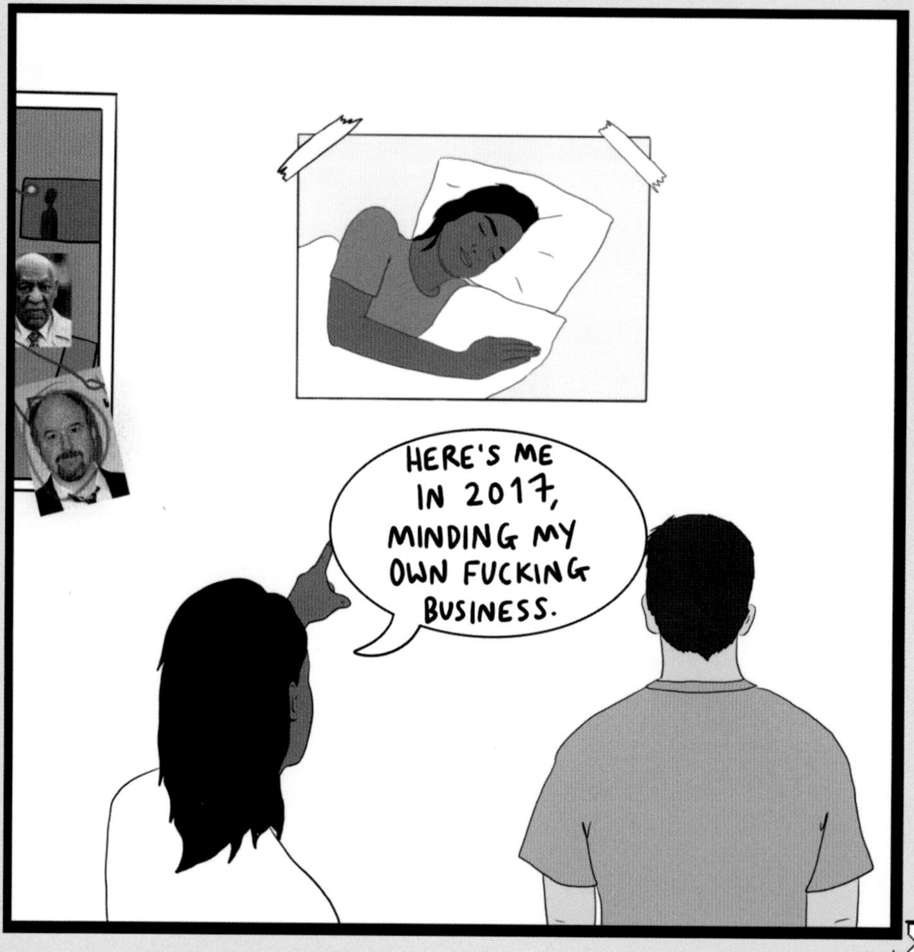
HERE'S ME IN 2017, MINDING MY OWN FUCKING BUSINESS.

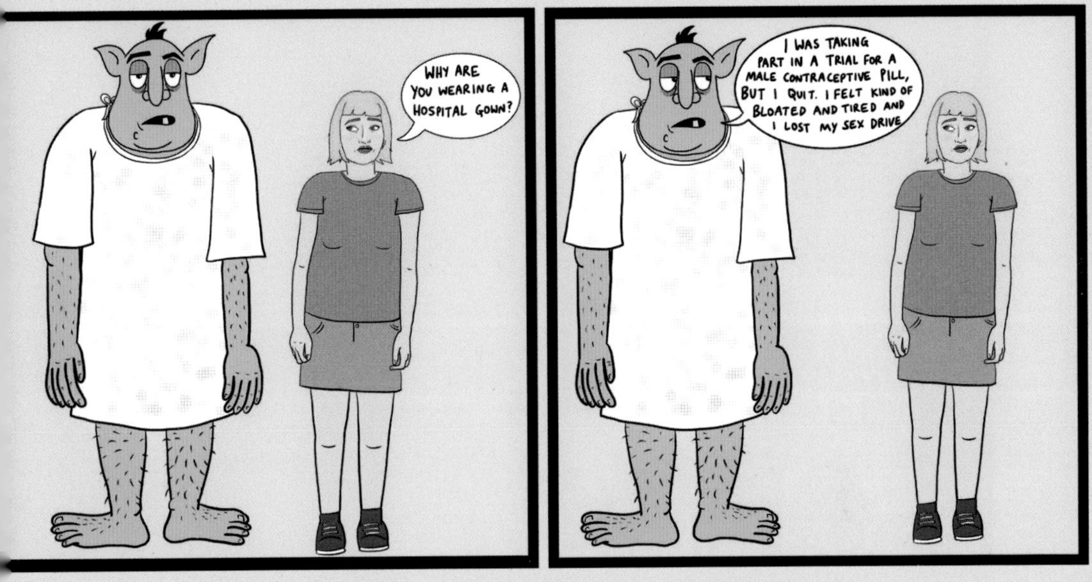
WHY ARE YOU WEARING A HOSPITAL GOWN?
I WAS TAKING PART IN A TRIAL FOR A MALE CONTRACEPTIVE PILL, BUT I QUIT. I FELT KIND OF BLOATED AND TIRED AND I LOST MY SEX DRIVE

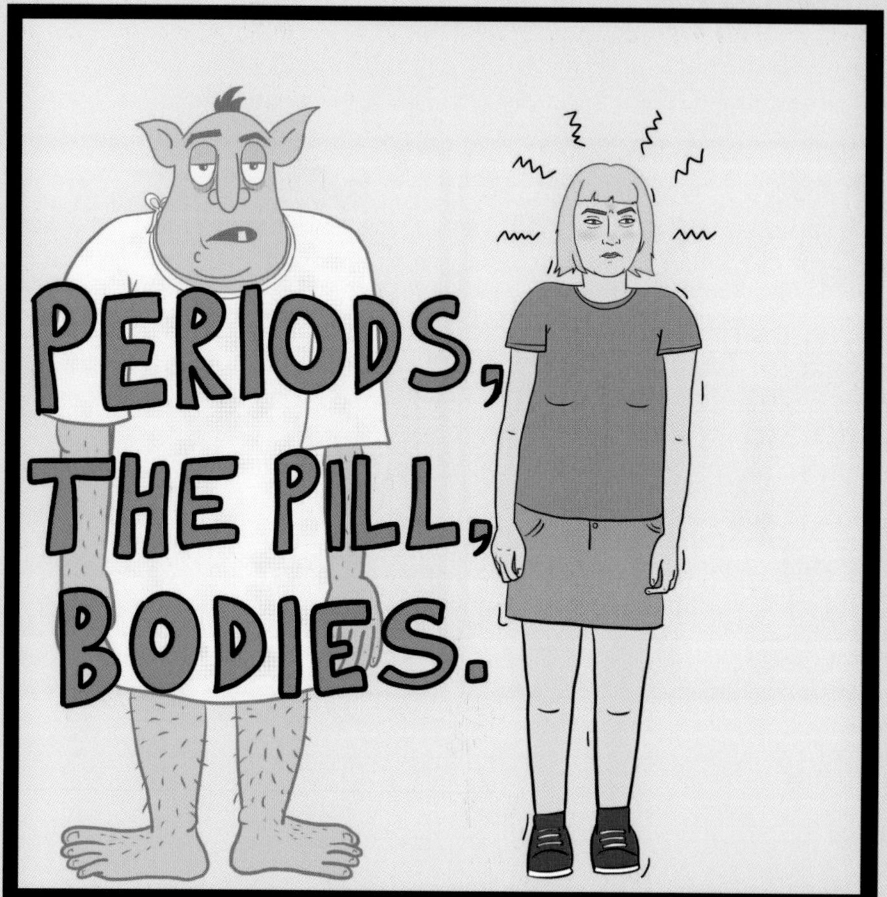
PERIODS,
THE PILL,
BODIES.

INSIDE OUT 2

THE MENSTRUAL CYCLE

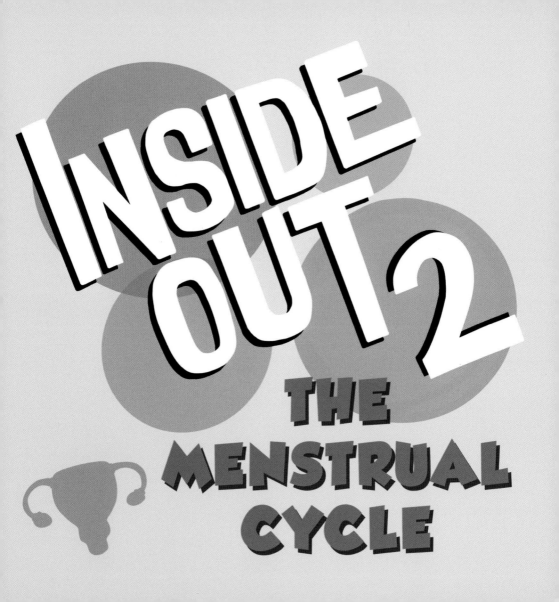

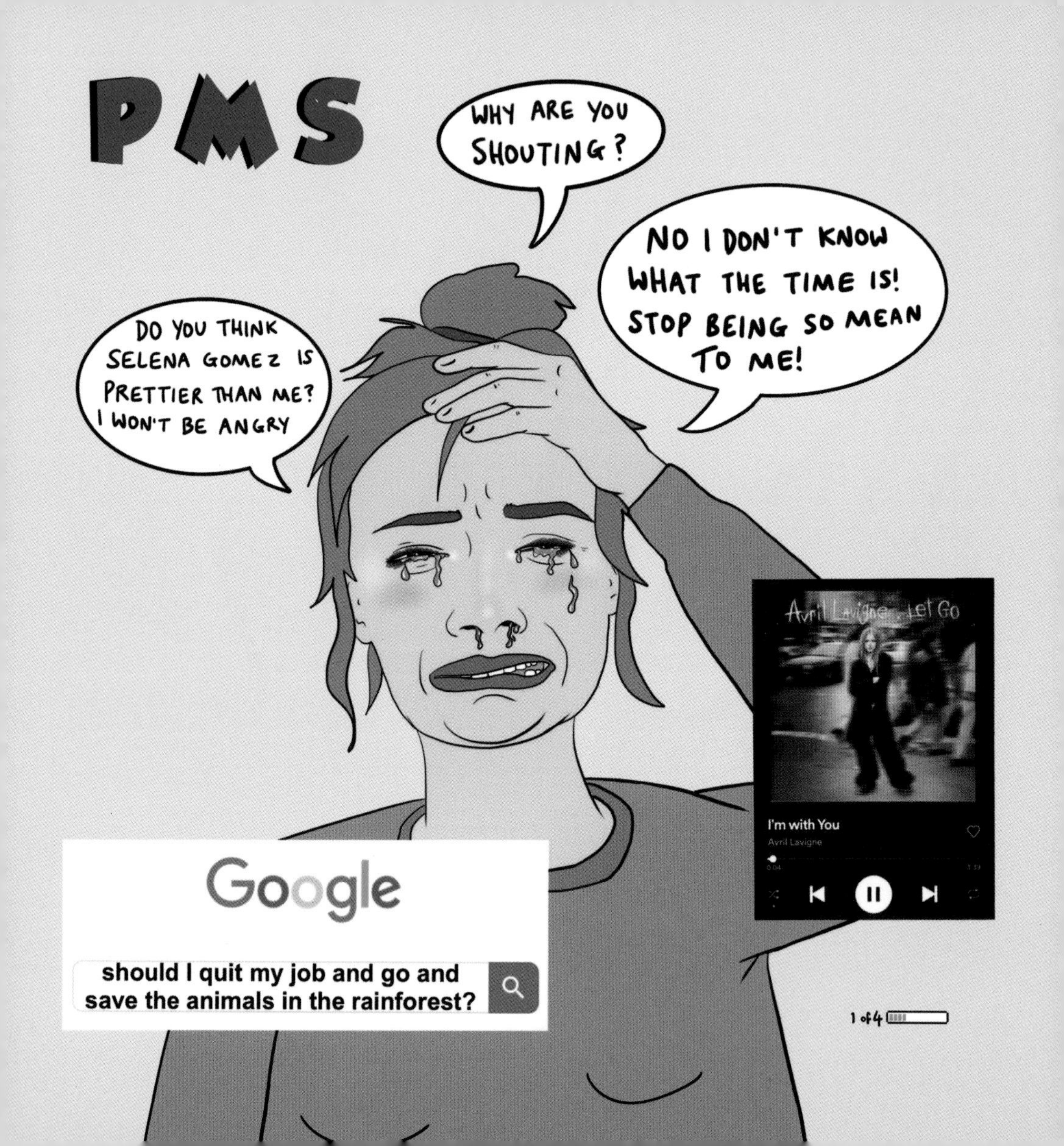
PMS
WHY ARE YOU SHOUTING?
NO I DON'T KNOW WHAT THE TIME IS! STOP BEING SO MEAN TO ME!
DO YOU THINK SELENA GOMEZ IS PRETTIER THAN ME? I WON'T BE ANGRY
Avril Lavigne Let Go
I'm with You
Avril Lavigne
Google
should I quit my job and go and save the animals in the rainforest?
1 of 4

ON YOUR PERIOD

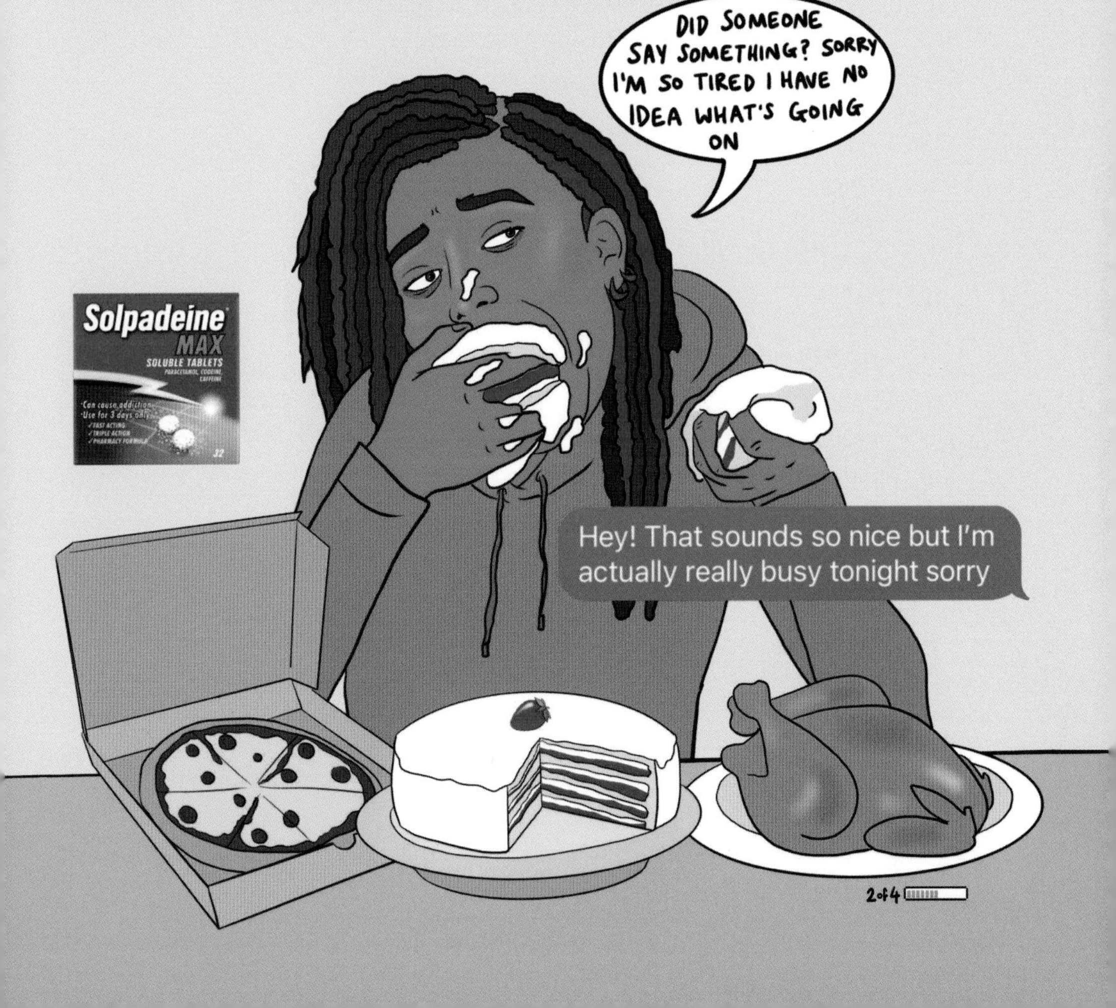
DID SOMEONE SAY SOMETHING? SORRY I'M SO TIRED I HAVE NO IDEA WHAT'S GOING ON
Solpadeine MAX
SOLUBLE TABLETS
Can cause addiction
Use for 3 days only
32
Hey! That sounds so nice but I'm actually really busy tonight sorry
2 of 4

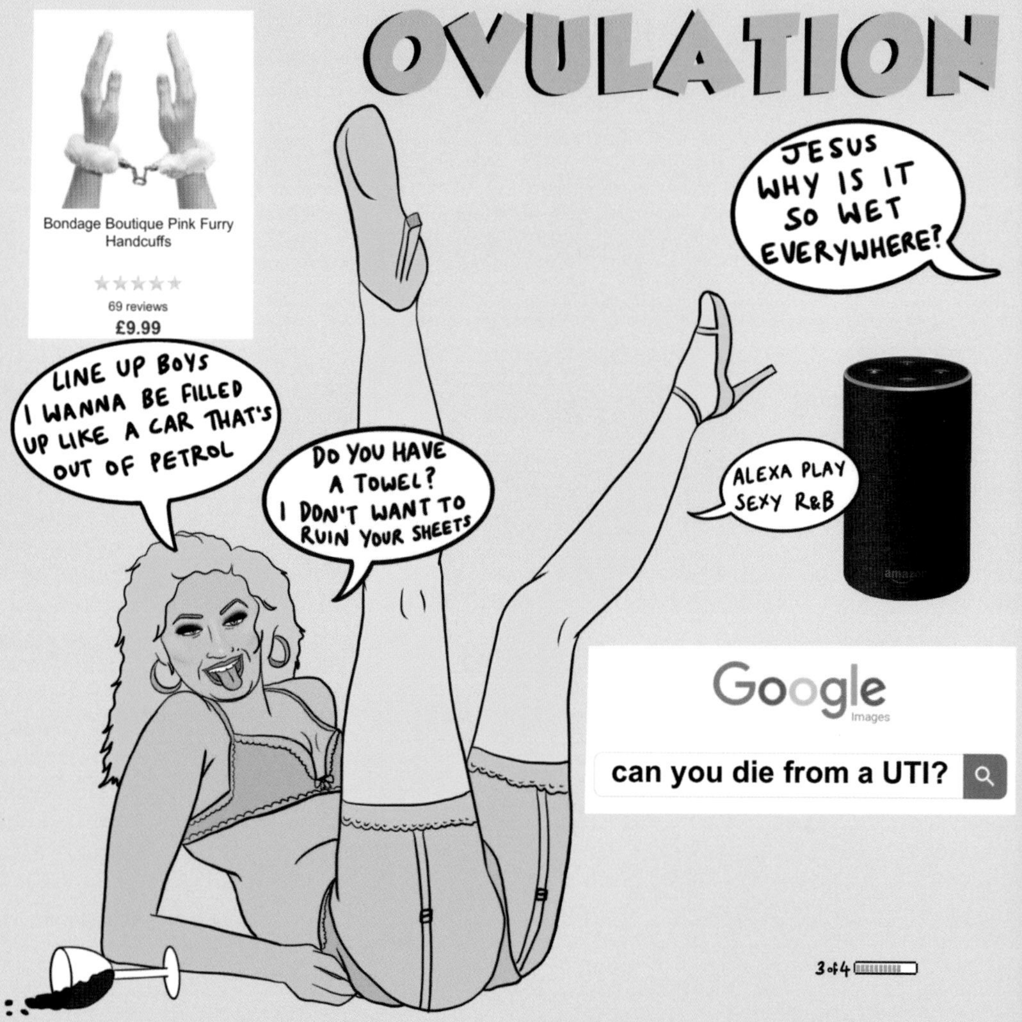

OVULATION
Bondage Boutique Pink Furry Handcuffs
69 reviews
£9.99
LINE UP BOYS I WANNA BE FILLED UP LIKE A CAR THAT'S OUT OF PETROL
DO YOU HAVE A TOWEL? I DON'T WANT TO RUIN YOUR SHEETS
JESUS WHY IS IT SO WET EVERYWHERE?
ALEXA PLAY SEXY R&B
Google Images
can you die from a UTI?
3 of 4

THE REST OF THE MONTH

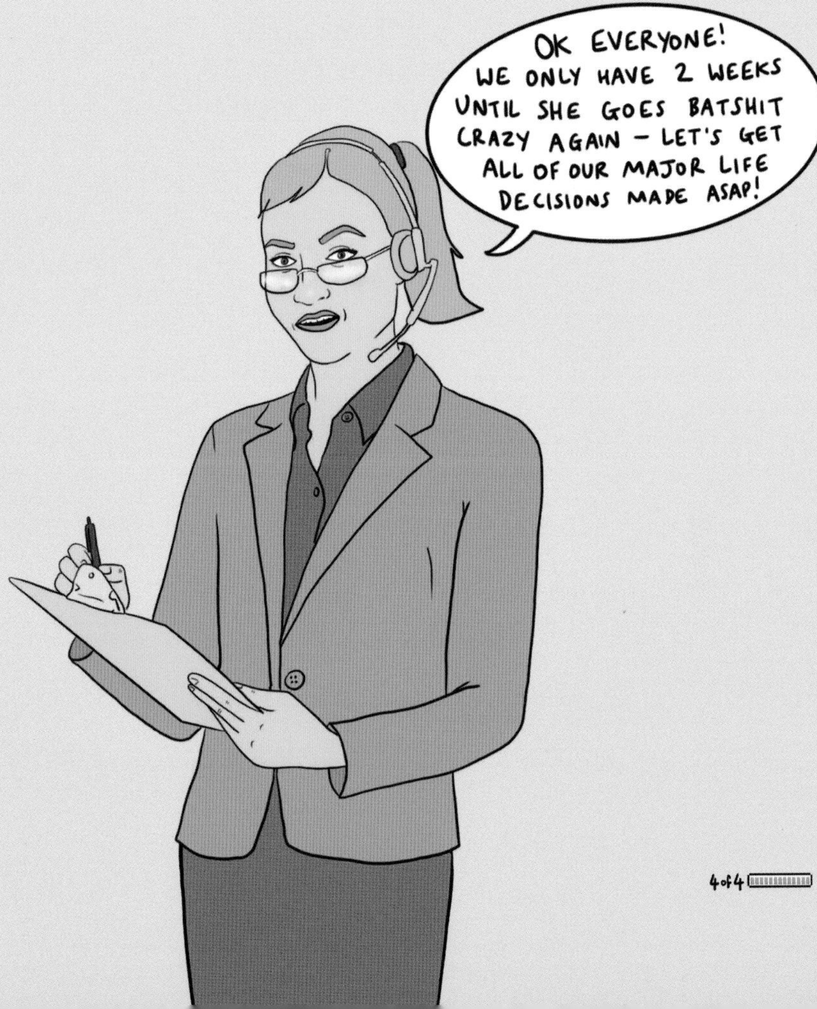
OK EVERYONE! WE ONLY HAVE 2 WEEKS UNTIL SHE GOES BATSHIT CRAZY AGAIN – LET'S GET ALL OF OUR MAJOR LIFE DECISIONS MADE ASAP!
4 of 4

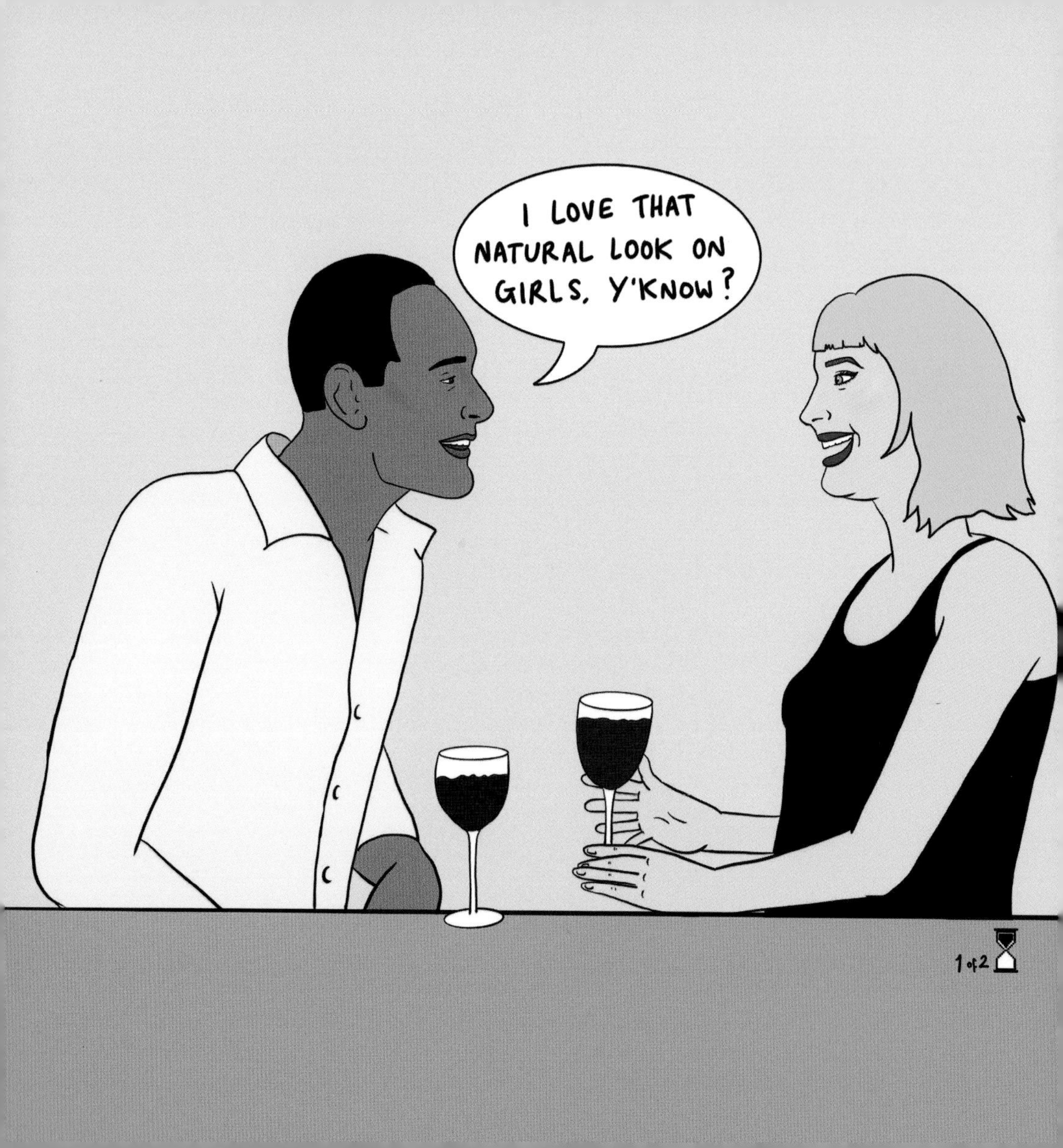
I LOVE THAT NATURAL LOOK ON GIRLS, Y'KNOW?
1 of 2

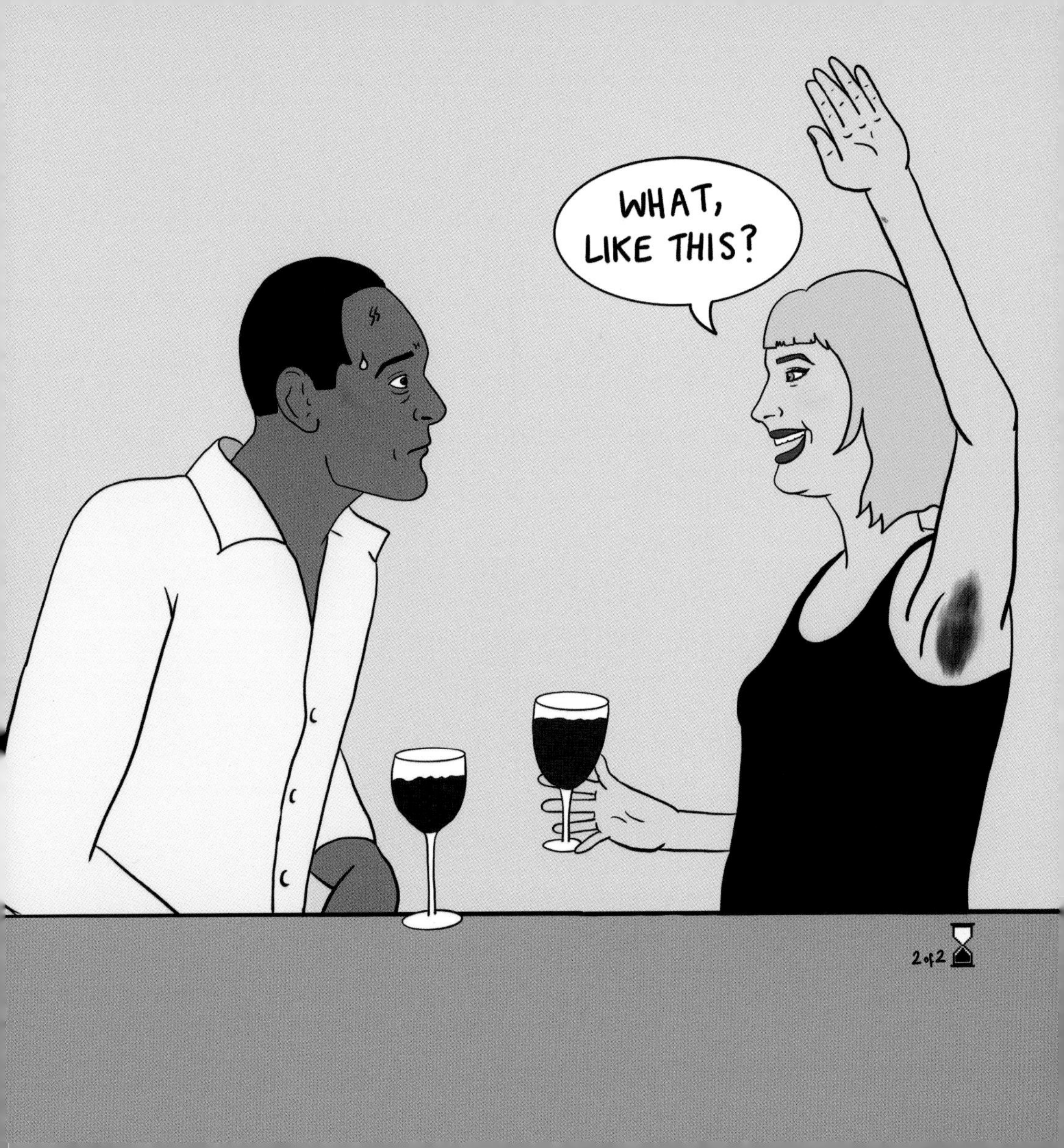
WHAT, LIKE THIS?
2 of 2

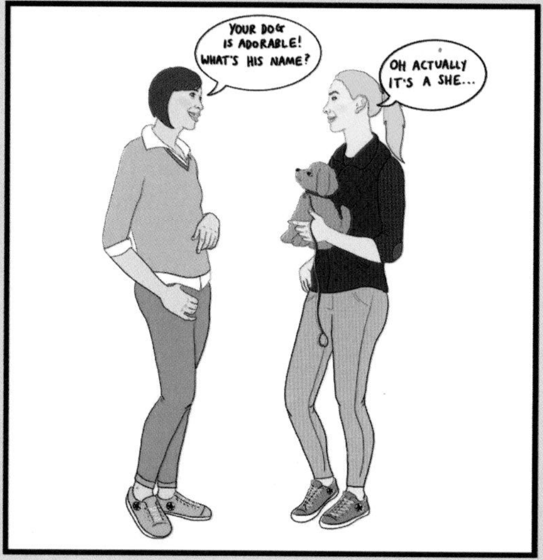
YOUR DOG IS ADORABLE! WHAT'S HIS NAME?
OH ACTUALLY IT'S A SHE...

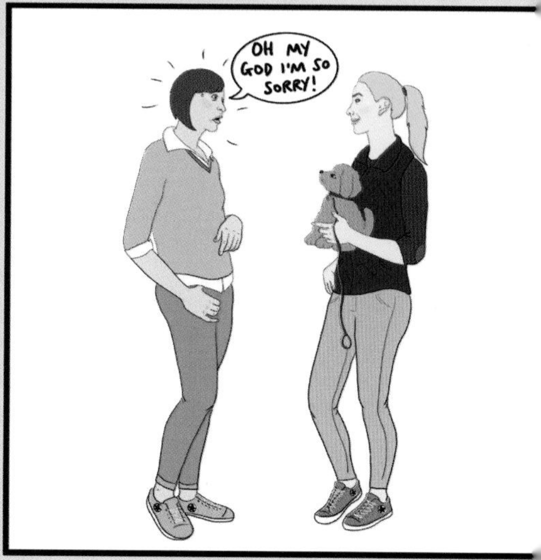
OH MY GOD I'M SO SORRY!

1 of 4

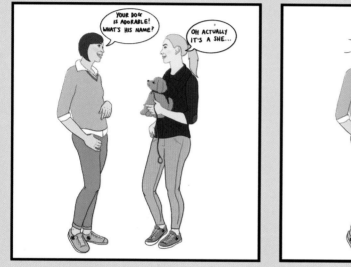

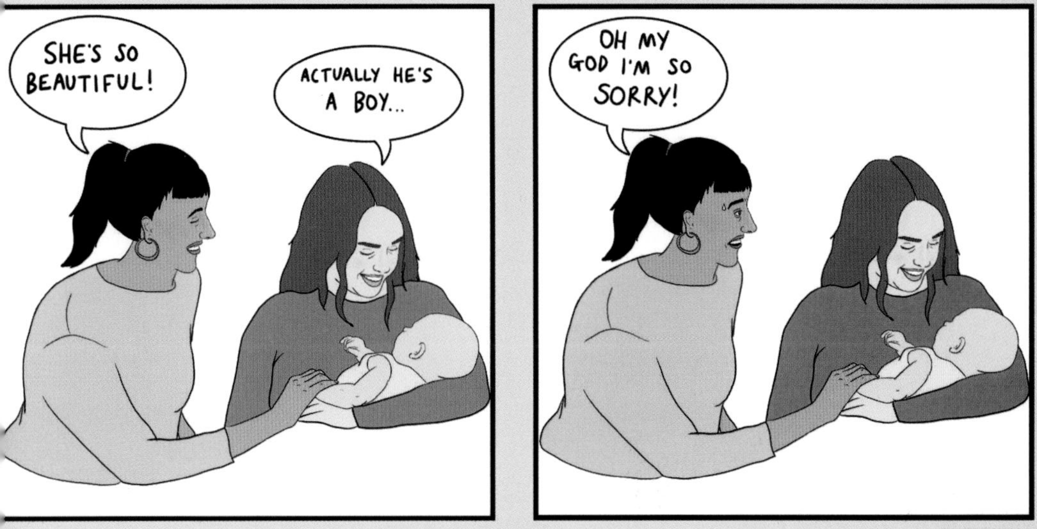
SHE'S SO BEAUTIFUL!
ACTUALLY HE'S A BOY...
OH MY GOD I'M SO SORRY!

2 of 4

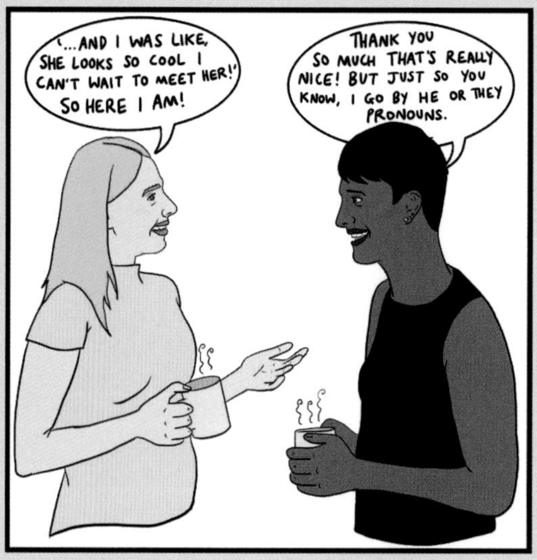
'...AND I WAS LIKE, SHE LOOKS SO COOL I CAN'T WAIT TO MEET HER!' SO HERE I AM!
THANK YOU SO MUCH THAT'S REALLY NICE! BUT JUST SO YOU KNOW, I GO BY HE OR THEY PRONOUNS.

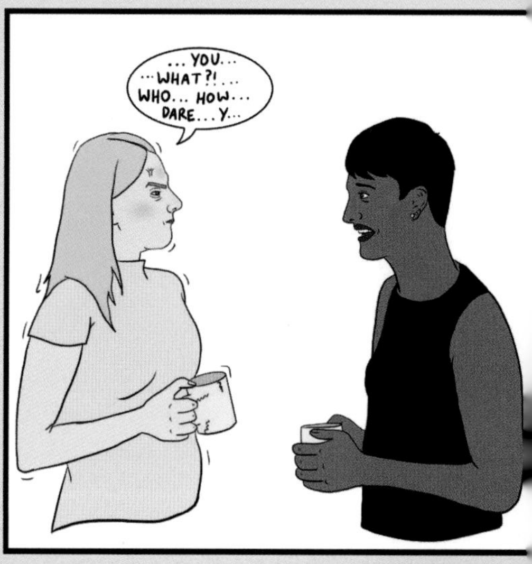
... YOU... ...WHAT?!... WHO... HOW... DARE... Y...

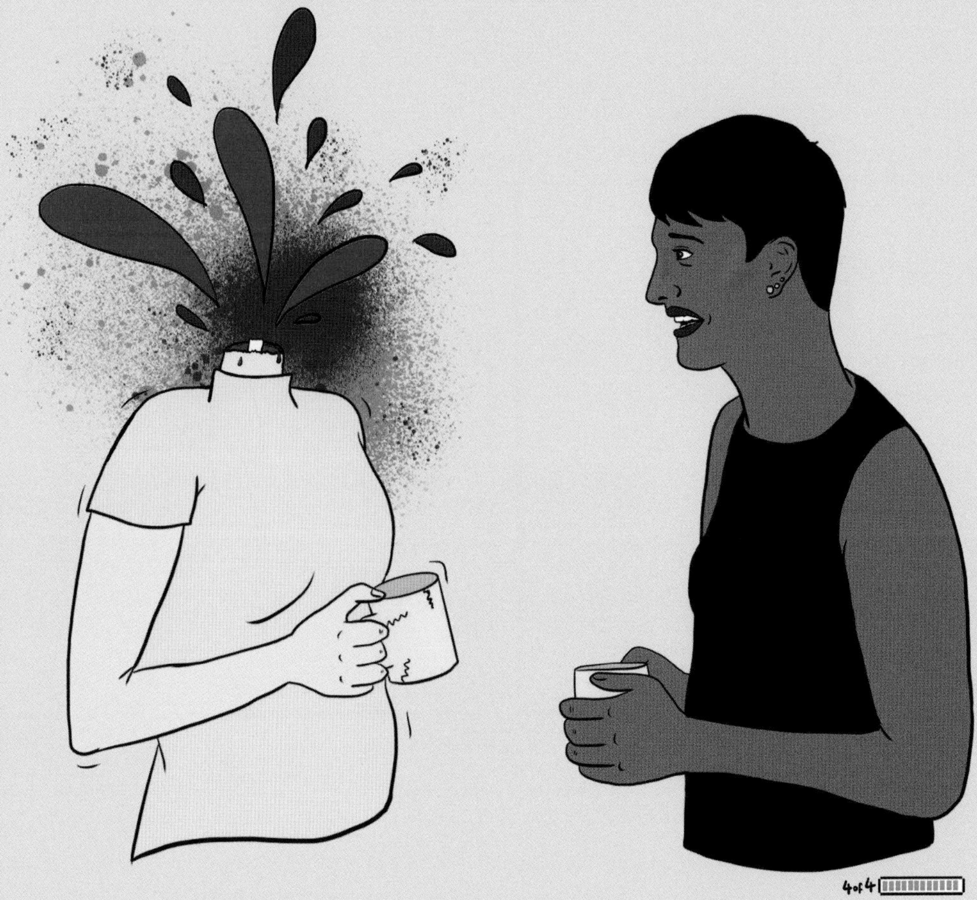
4 of 4

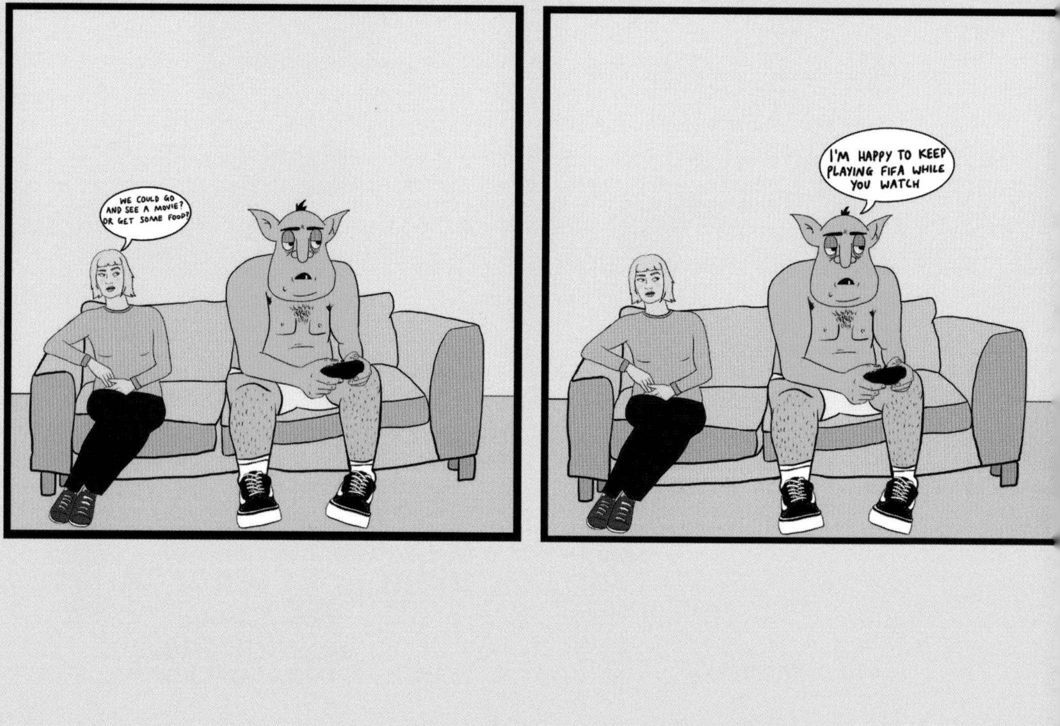
WE COULD GO AND SEE A MOVIE? OR GET SOME FOOD?
I'M HAPPY TO KEEP PLAYING FIFA WHILE YOU WATCH

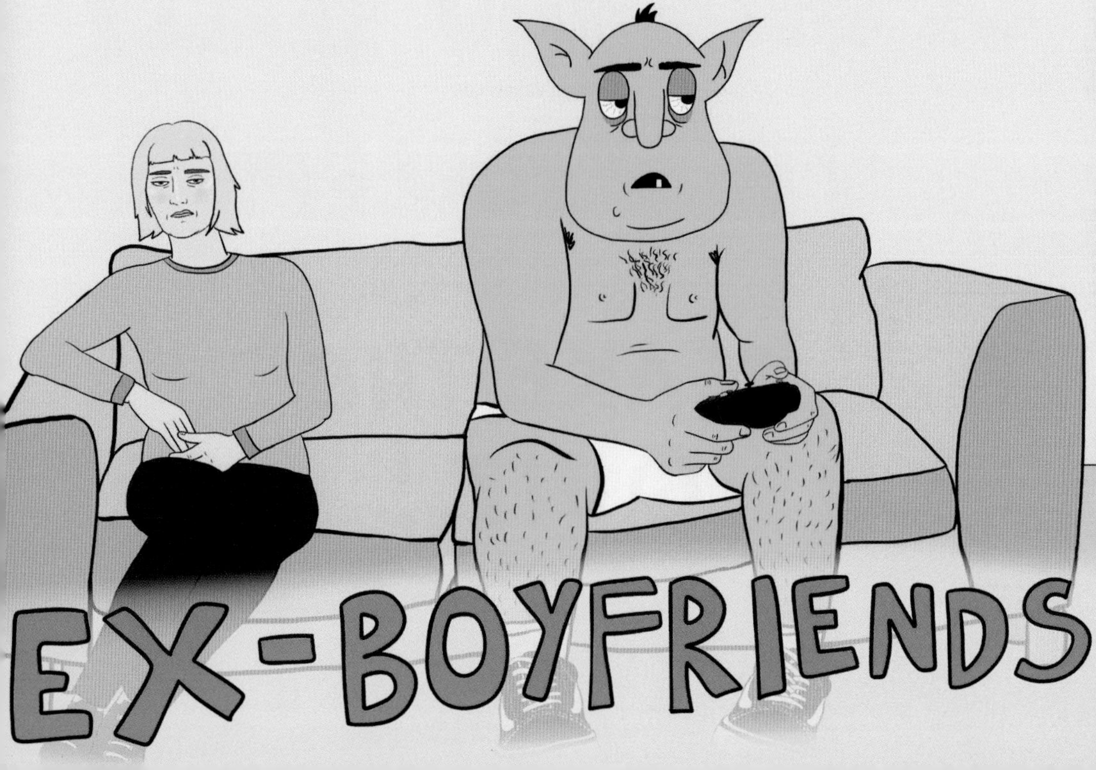

EX-BOYFRIENDS

WAS YOUR EX-GIRLFRIEND ACTUALLY CRAZY OR WERE YOU REALLY THE PROBLEM?

TAKE THE QUIZ!

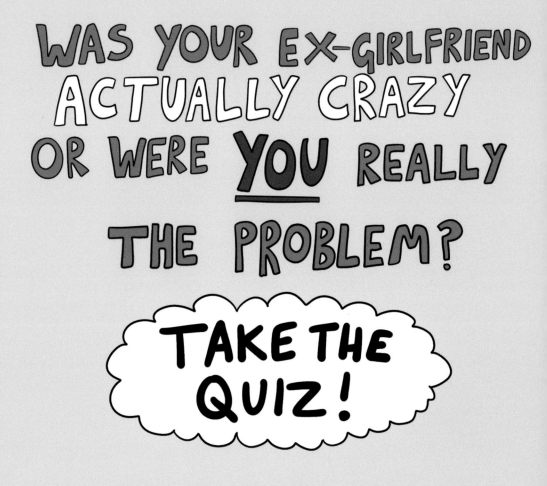

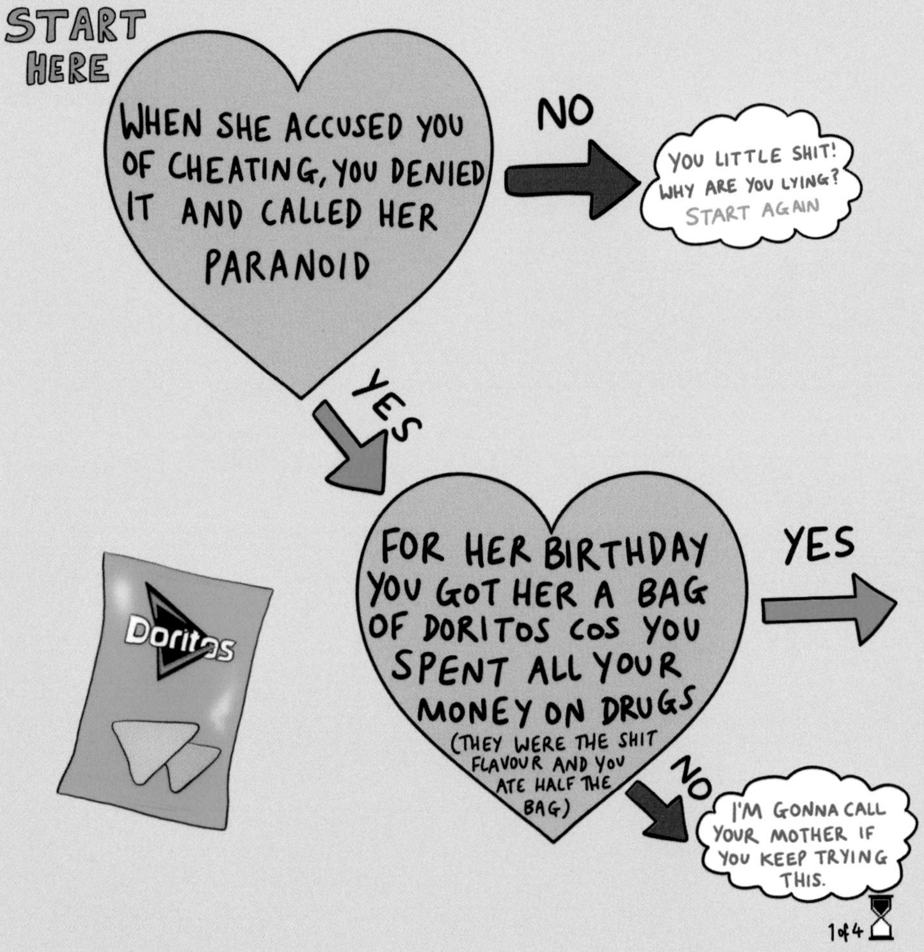

START HERE
WHEN SHE ACCUSED YOU OF CHEATING, YOU DENIED IT AND CALLED HER PARANOID
NO
YOU LITTLE SHIT! WHY ARE YOU LYING? START AGAIN
YES
FOR HER BIRTHDAY YOU GOT HER A BAG OF DORITOS COS YOU SPENT ALL YOUR MONEY ON DRUGS
(THEY WERE THE SHIT FLAVOUR AND YOU ATE HALF THE BAG)
YES
NO
I'M GONNA CALL YOUR MOTHER IF YOU KEEP TRYING THIS.
Doritos
1 of 4

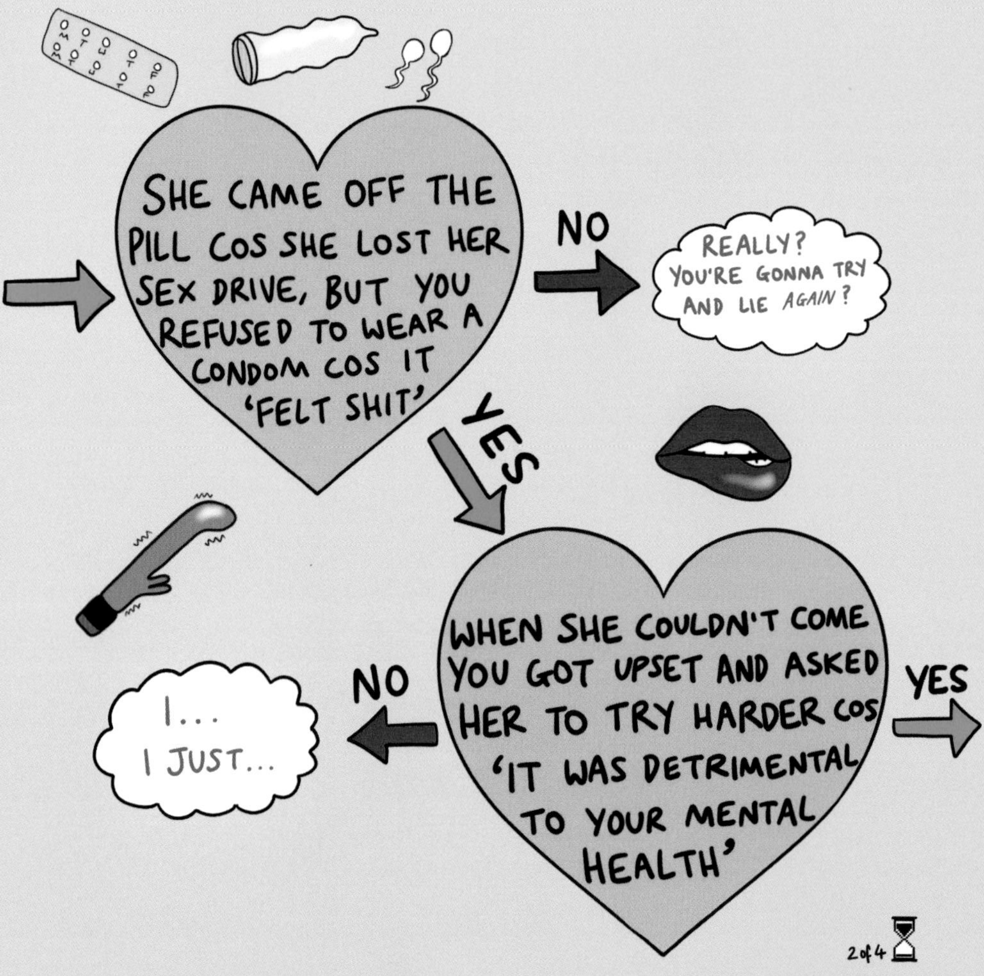
SHE CAME OFF THE PILL COS SHE LOST HER SEX DRIVE, BUT YOU REFUSED TO WEAR A CONDOM COS IT 'FELT SHIT'
NO
REALLY? YOU'RE GONNA TRY AND LIE AGAIN?
YES
WHEN SHE COULDN'T COME YOU GOT UPSET AND ASKED HER TO TRY HARDER COS 'IT WAS DETRIMENTAL TO YOUR MENTAL HEALTH'
NO
I...
I JUST...
YES
2 of 4

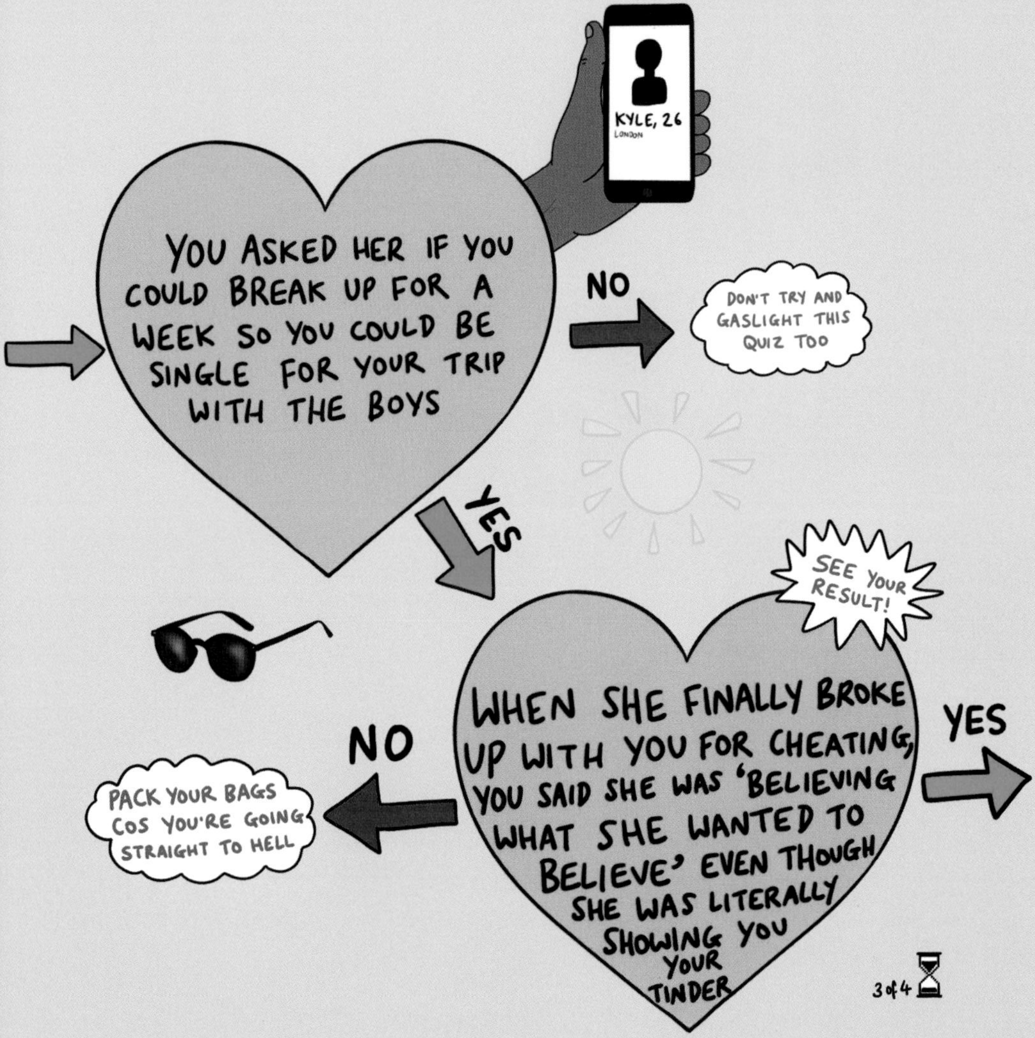

KYLE, 26
LONDON
YOU ASKED HER IF YOU COULD BREAK UP FOR A WEEK SO YOU COULD BE SINGLE FOR YOUR TRIP WITH THE BOYS
NO
DON'T TRY AND GASLIGHT THIS QUIZ TOO
YES
SEE YOUR RESULT!
WHEN SHE FINALLY BROKE UP WITH YOU FOR CHEATING, YOU SAID SHE WAS 'BELIEVING WHAT SHE WANTED TO BELIEVE' EVEN THOUGH SHE WAS LITERALLY SHOWING YOU YOUR TINDER
NO
PACK YOUR BAGS COS YOU'RE GOING STRAIGHT TO HELL
YES
3 of 4

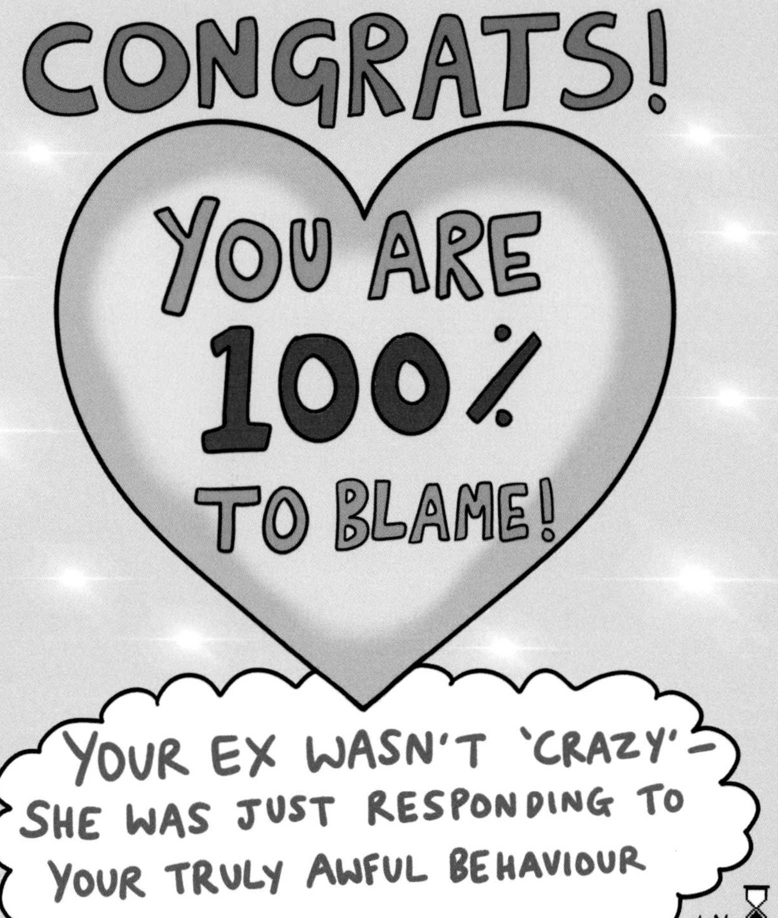
CONGRATS!
YOU ARE 100% TO BLAME!
YOUR EX WASN'T 'CRAZY' — SHE WAS JUST RESPONDING TO YOUR TRULY AWFUL BEHAVIOUR
4 of 4

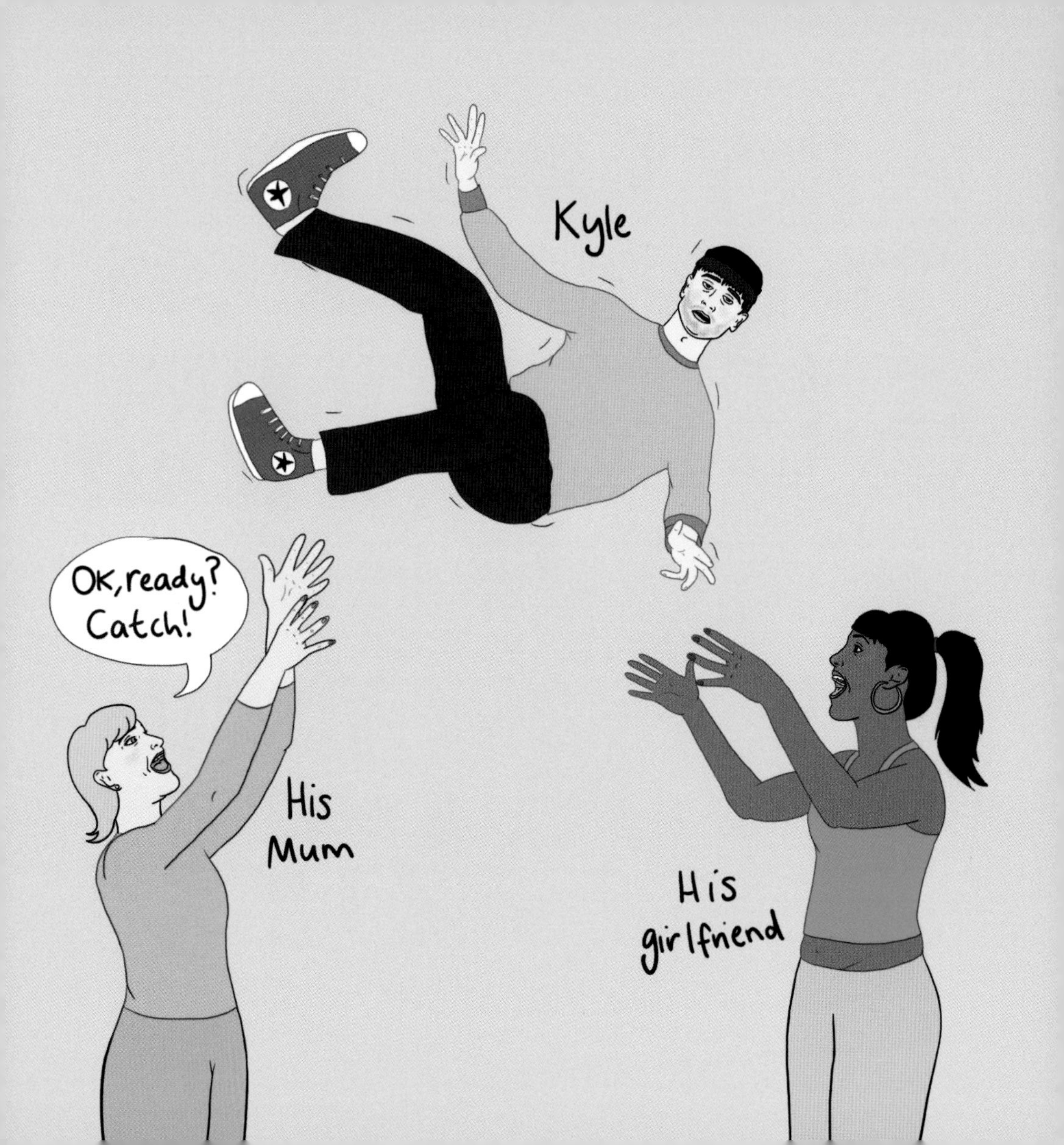
Kyle
Ok, ready? Catch!
His Mum
His girlfriend

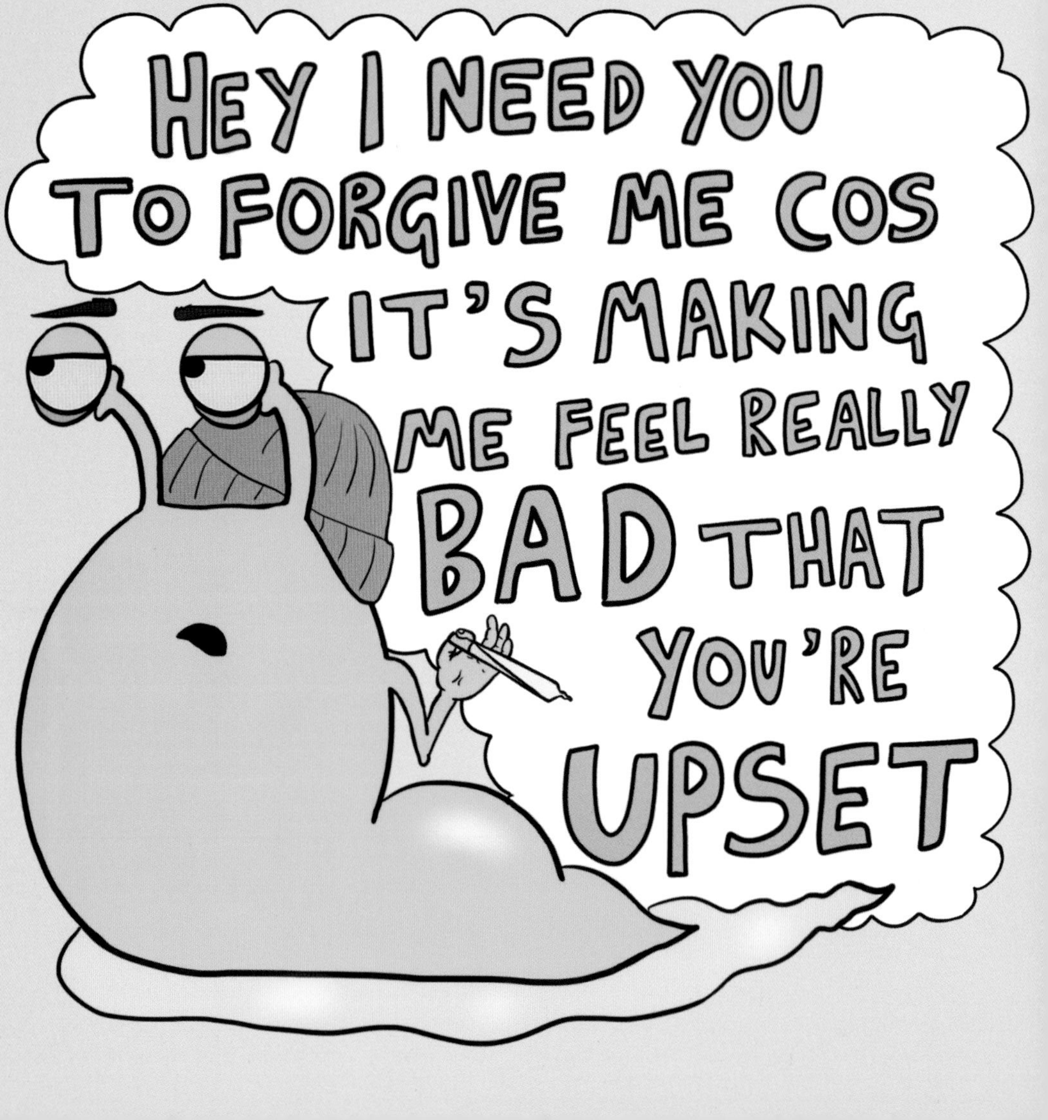
HEY I NEED YOU TO FORGIVE ME COS IT'S MAKING ME FEEL REALLY BAD THAT YOU'RE UPSET

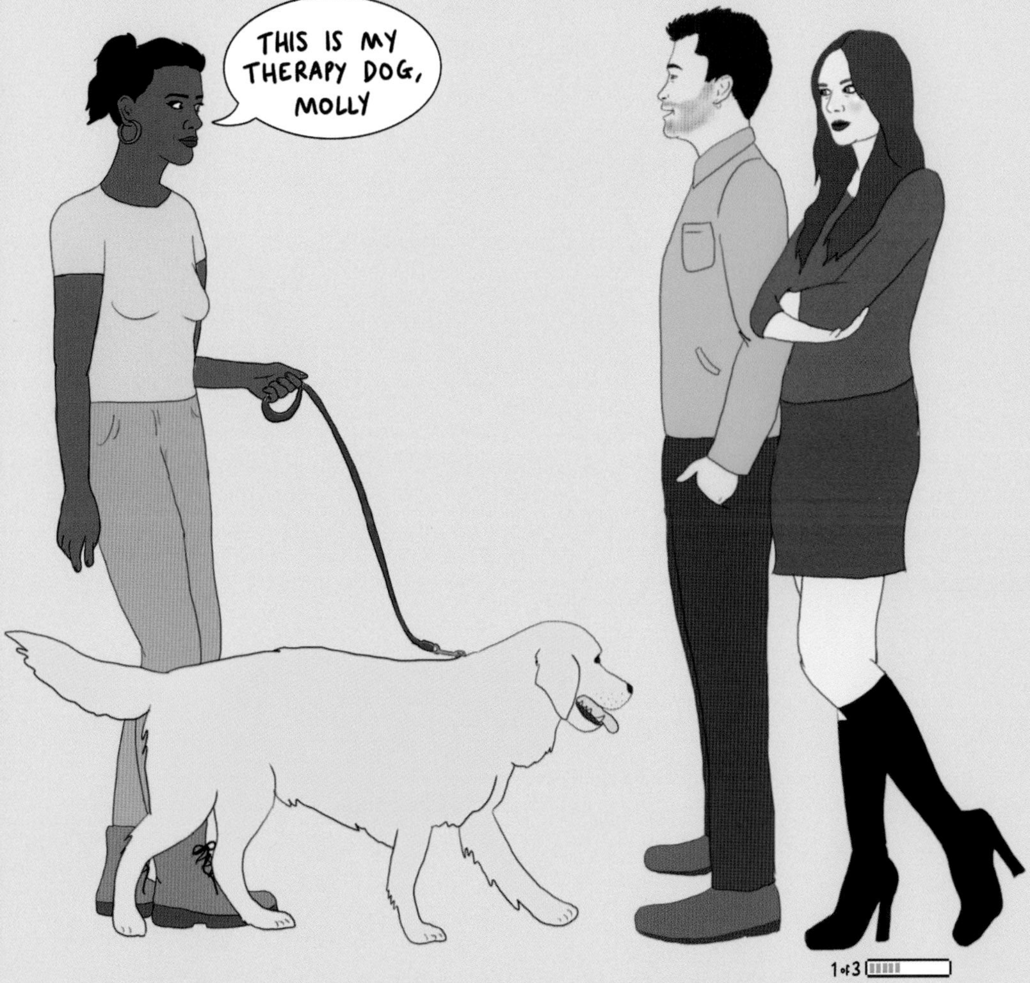
THIS IS MY THERAPY DOG, MOLLY
1 of 3

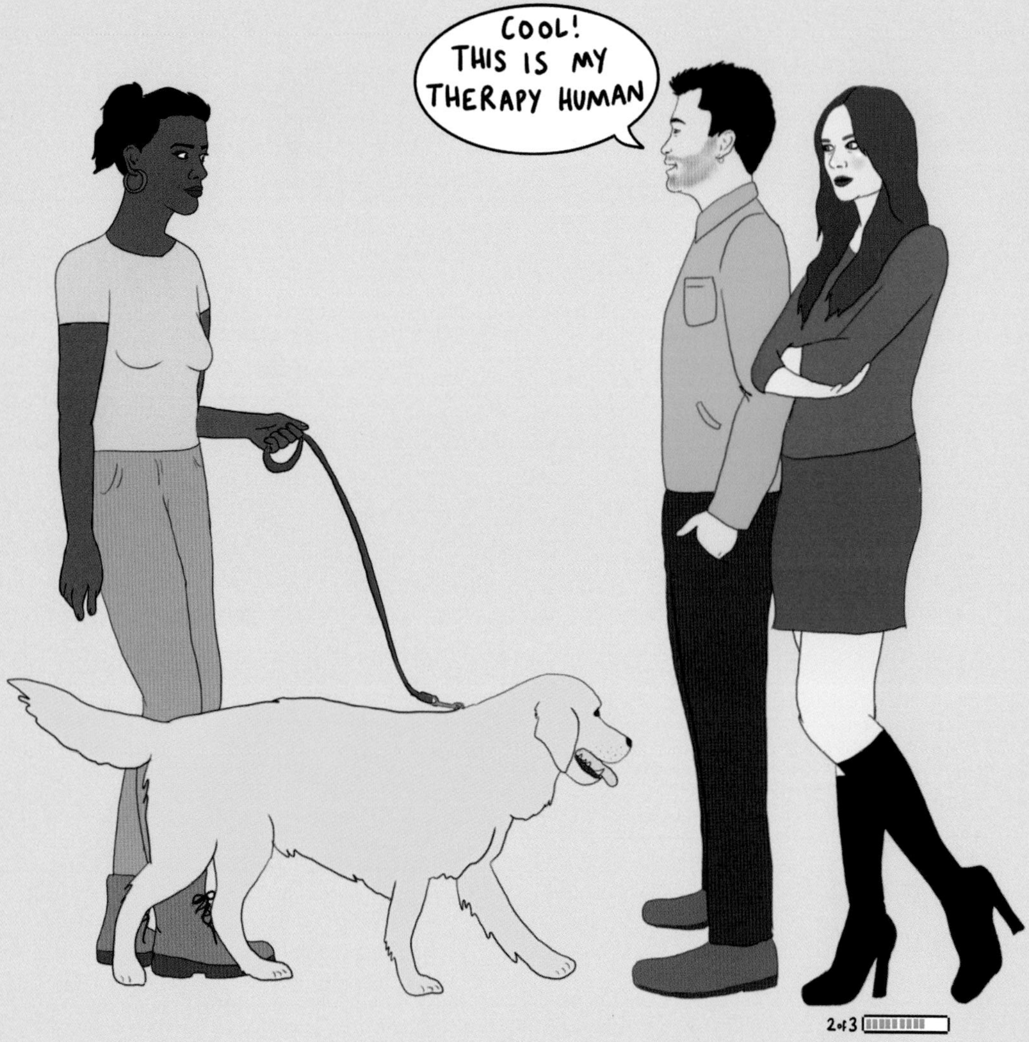
COOL! THIS IS MY THERAPY HUMAN
2 of 3

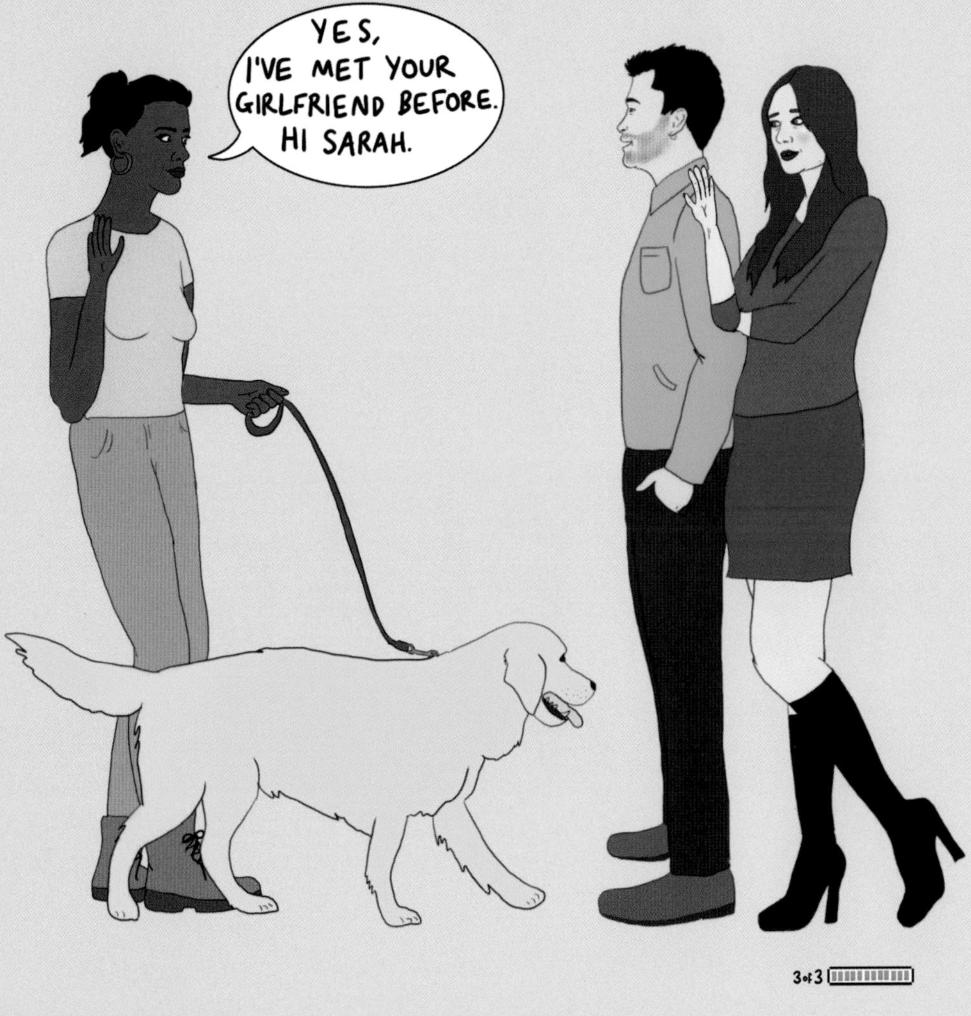
YES,
I'VE MET YOUR
GIRLFRIEND BEFORE.
HI SARAH.
3of3

THREE ADORABLE D.I.Y PROJECTS TO MAKE FROM THE RED FLAGS HE GIVES YOU

ARTS AND CRAFTS ARE SO SOOTHING!

TIME TO GRAB YOUR GLITTER AND GLUE!

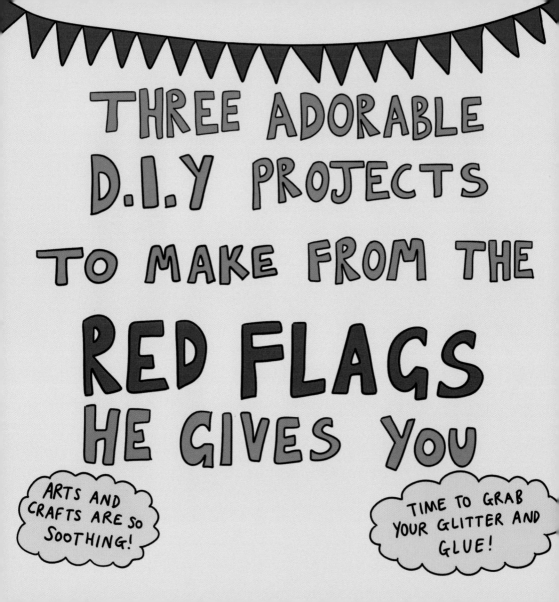

1

A DRESS HE'LL ASK YOU NOT TO WEAR COS IT'S 'TOO SLUTTY'

2

A MAP COS HE'S ALWAYS ASKING WHERE YOU ARE

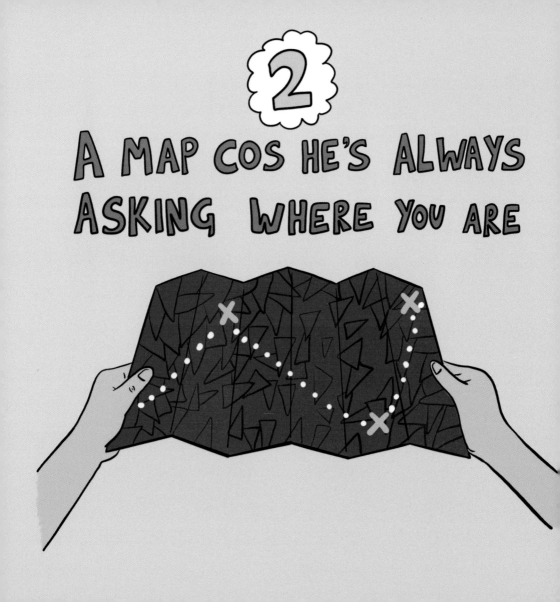

3

A HEART PAPER CHAIN
TO GIVE TO THE WAITER
HE MADE CRY

SORRY ABOUT HIM

BONUS!

WHEN YOU FINALLY GET RID OF HIM, USE ANY LEFTOVER **RED FLAGS** TO MAKE A HEADDRESS FOR YOUR HINGE PICS

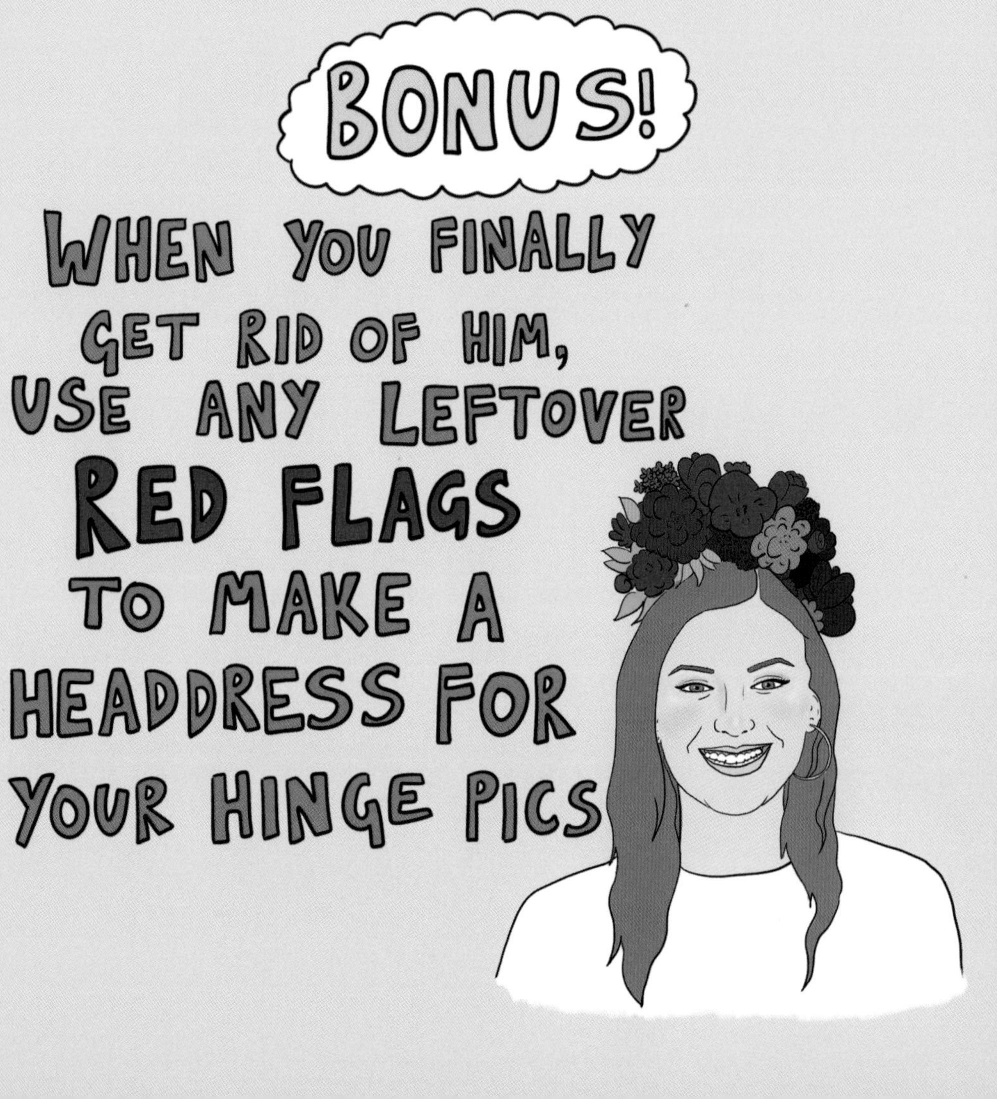

YOUR FIRST GIRLFRIEND: THE MACHINE!

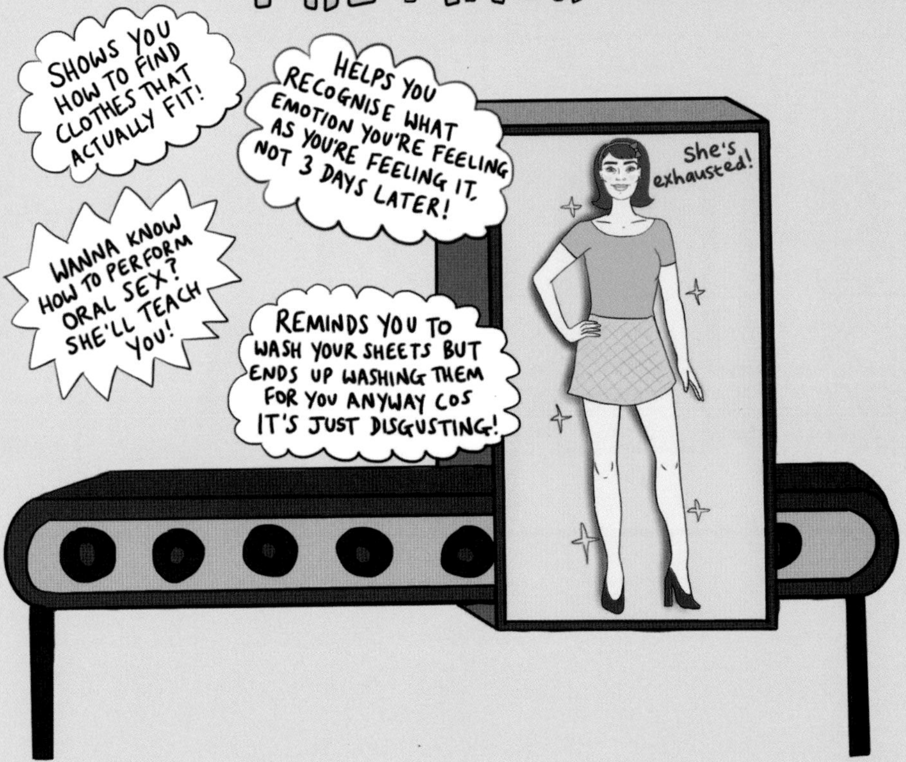
SHOWS YOU HOW TO FIND CLOTHES THAT ACTUALLY FIT!
HELPS YOU RECOGNISE WHAT EMOTION YOU'RE FEELING AS YOU'RE FEELING IT, NOT 3 DAYS LATER!
She's exhausted!
WANNA KNOW HOW TO PERFORM ORAL SEX? SHE'LL TEACH YOU!
REMINDS YOU TO WASH YOUR SHEETS BUT ENDS UP WASHING THEM FOR YOU ANYWAY COS IT'S JUST DISGUSTING!

1of 2

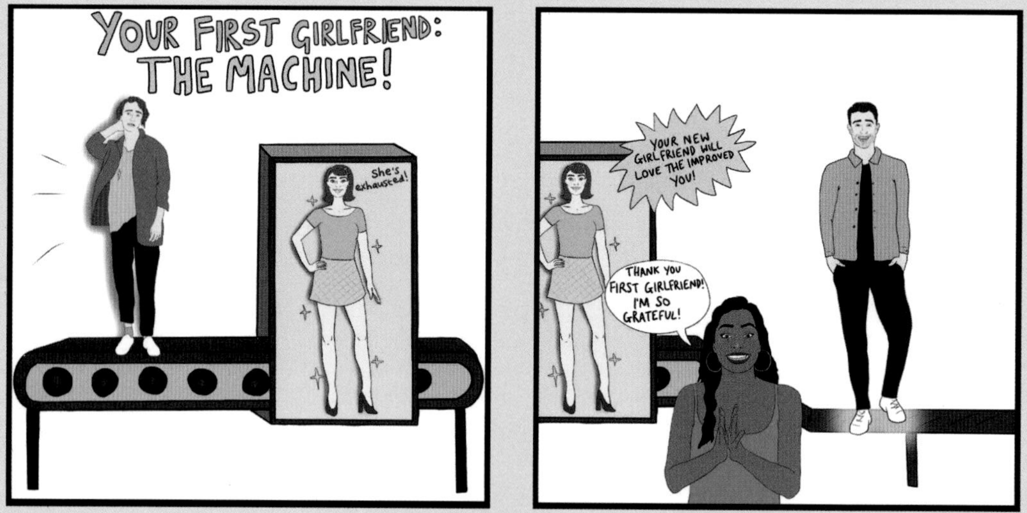
YOUR FIRST GIRLFRIEND: THE MACHINE!
She's exhausted!
YOUR NEW GIRLFRIEND WILL LOVE THE IMPROVED YOU!
THANK YOU FIRST GIRLFRIEND! I'M SO GRATEFUL!

2 of 2

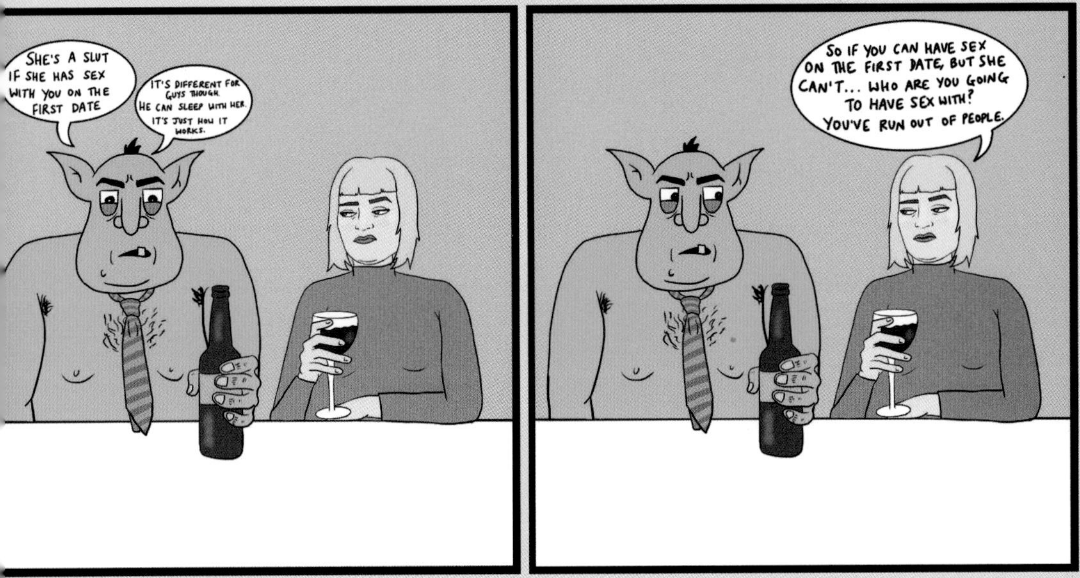
SHE'S A SLUT IF SHE HAS SEX WITH YOU ON THE FIRST DATE
IT'S DIFFERENT FOR GUYS THOUGH. HE CAN SLEEP WITH HER. IT'S JUST HOW IT WORKS.
SO IF YOU CAN HAVE SEX ON THE FIRST DATE, BUT SHE CAN'T... WHO ARE YOU GOING TO HAVE SEX WITH? YOU'VE RUN OUT OF PEOPLE.

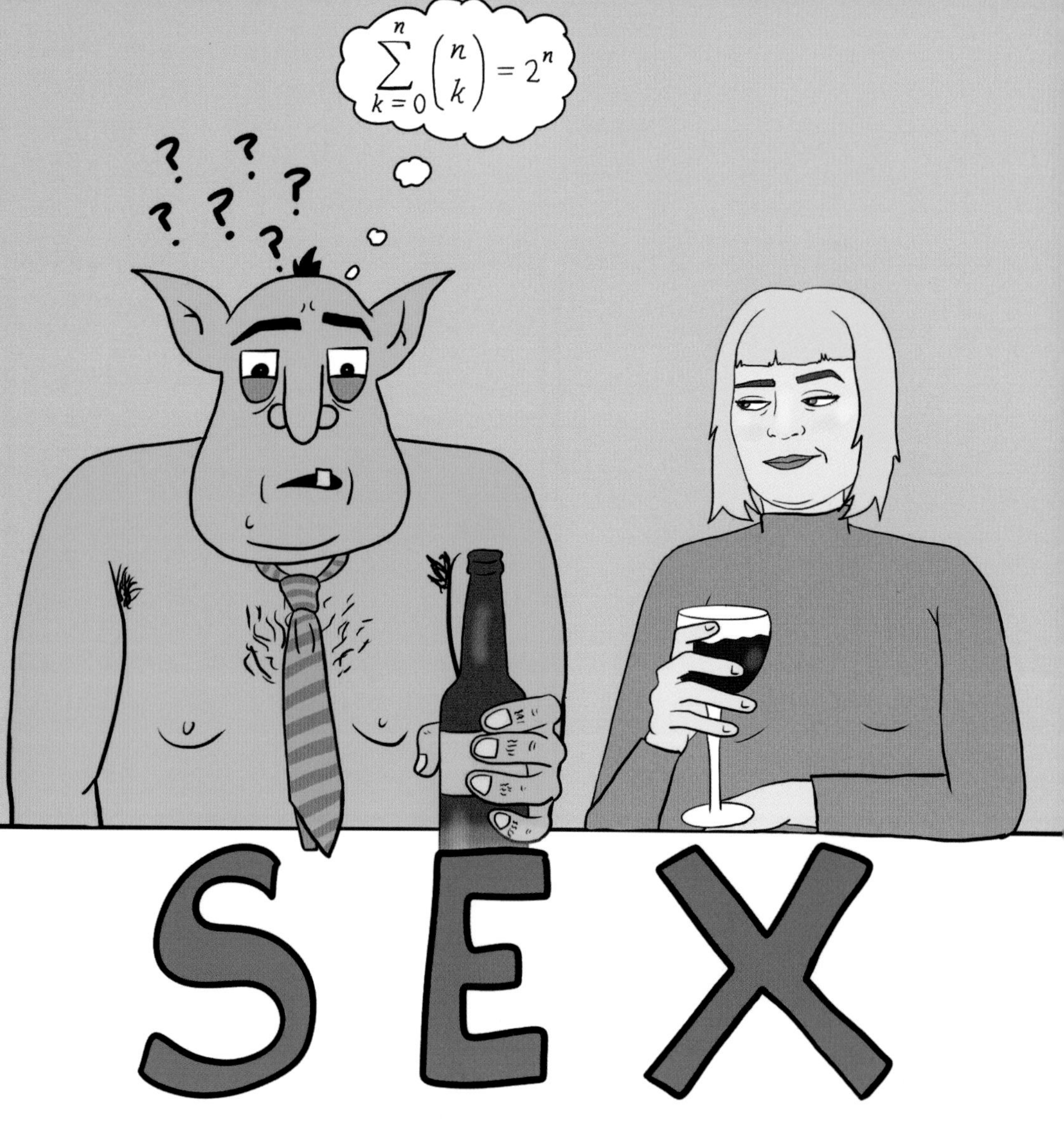
$\sum_{k=0}^{n}\binom{n}{k} = 2^n$
SEX

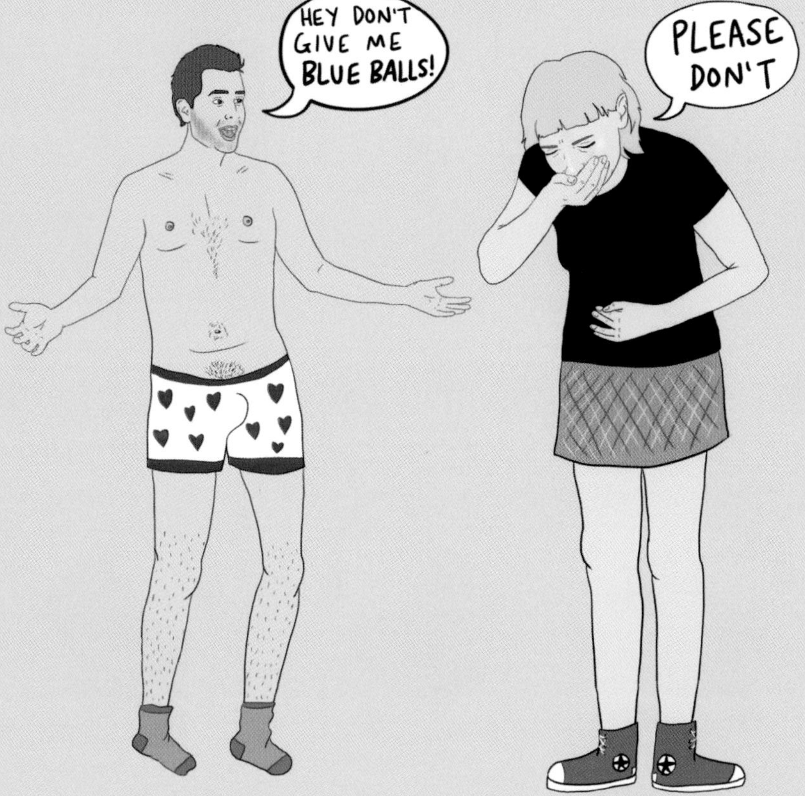
HEY DON'T GIVE ME BLUE BALLS!
PLEASE DON'T

WHY THE PHRASE 'BLUE BALLS' MAKES ME THROW UP IN MY MOUTH

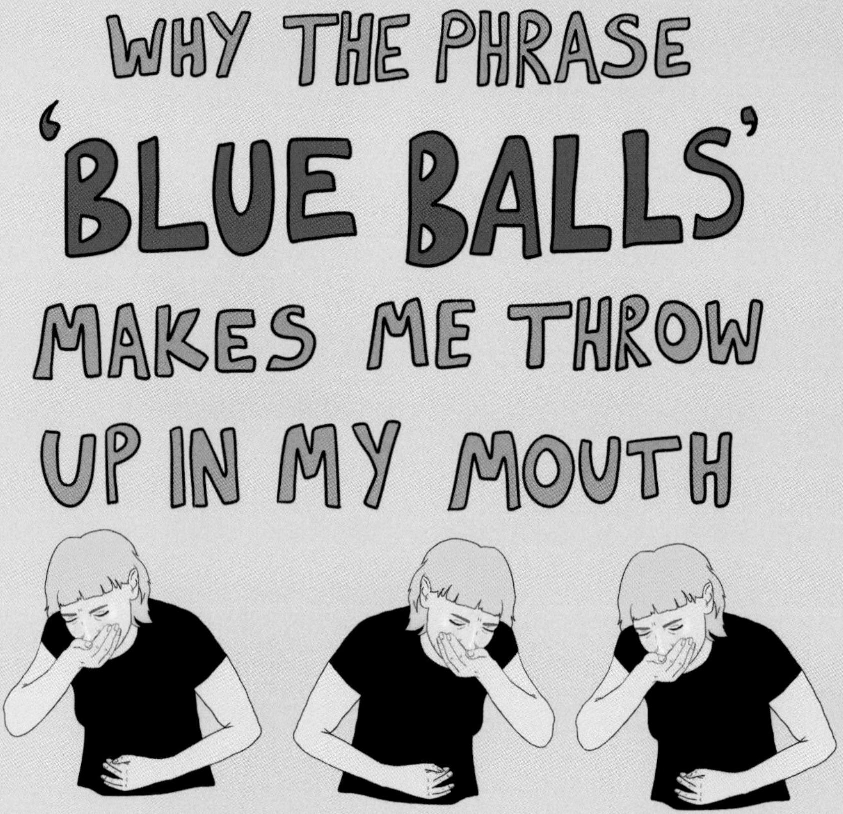

1. The phrase "HEY DON'T GIVE ME BLUE BALLS!" really means this:

'I'm asking you to perform a sexual act on me despite the fact that you've told me you don't want to.'

If the person you're fooling around with wants to stop, you stop. No questions asked.

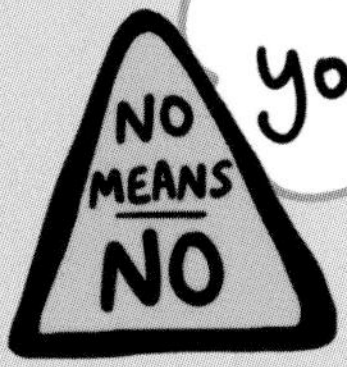
NO MEANS NO

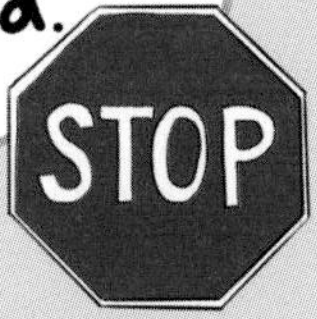
STOP

2. BLUE BALLS isn't exclusive to men.

- When someone is aroused, the blood flow to their genitals is increased. This causes an aching feeling, which goes away after an orgasm or after the arousal goes away.

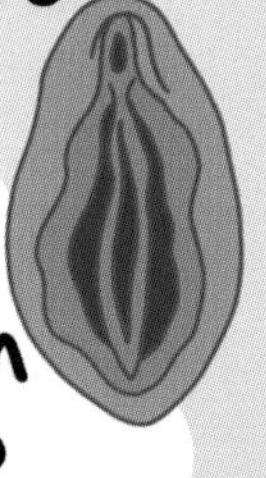

- "BLUE VULVA" is a thing. This phrase never caught on because women don't tend to rely on men to satisfy their needs.

3. The cure for blue balls isn't just coming. Distracting yourself makes the arousal go away and returns the blood flow back to normal.

Masturbate in private

Help an old person with their shopping

Play Fifa

THINGS TO MAKE YOUR BLUE BALLS GO AWAY THAT DON'T INVOLVE PRESSURING SOMEONE INTO SEX

Visit the Pyramids in Egypt

Call your Mum

Learn French

Plant a tree

Go for a walk

4. Why am I responsible for emptying your fluids?

ARE YOU A COW?

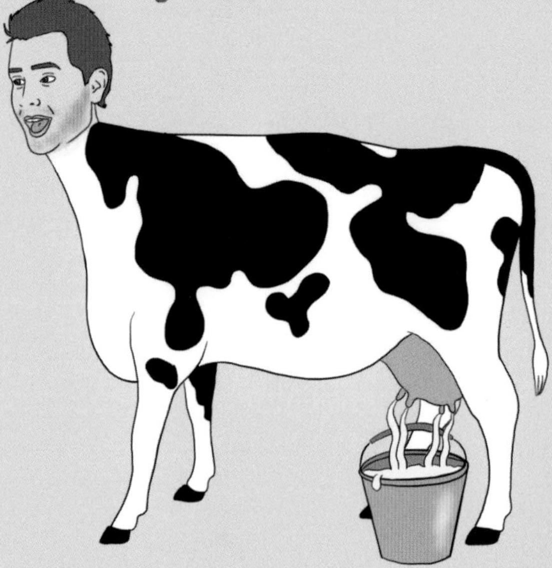

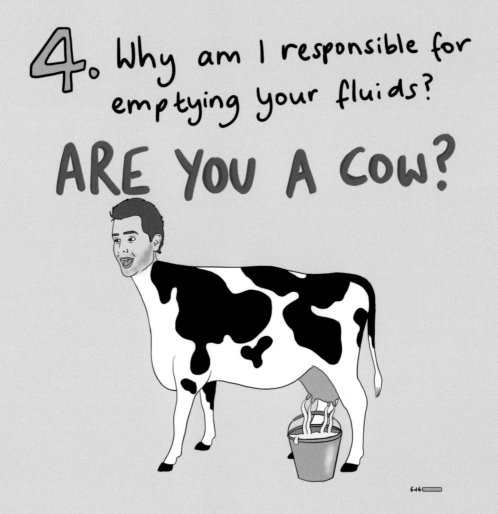

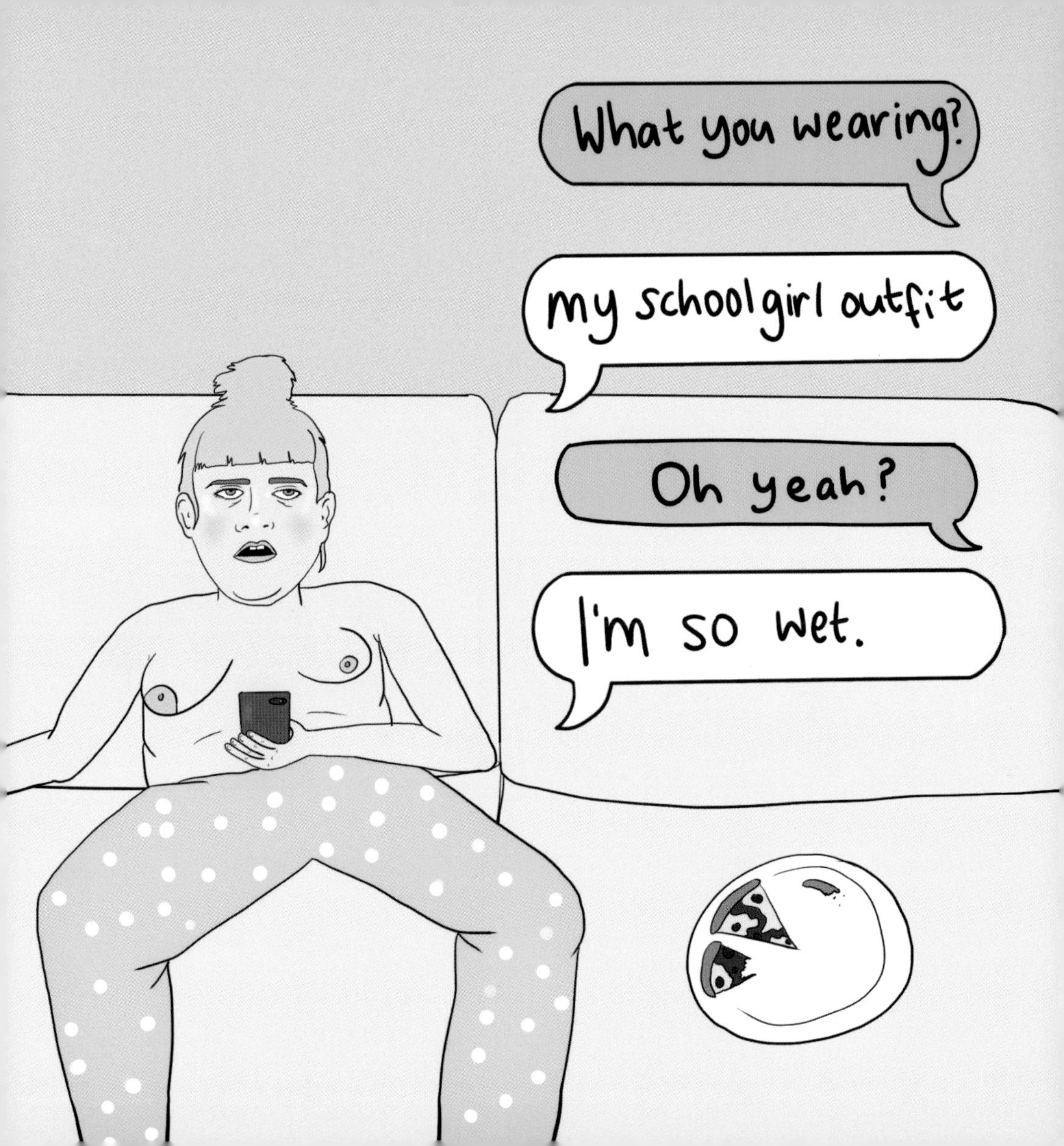
What you wearing?
my schoolgirl outfit
Oh yeah?
I'm so wet.

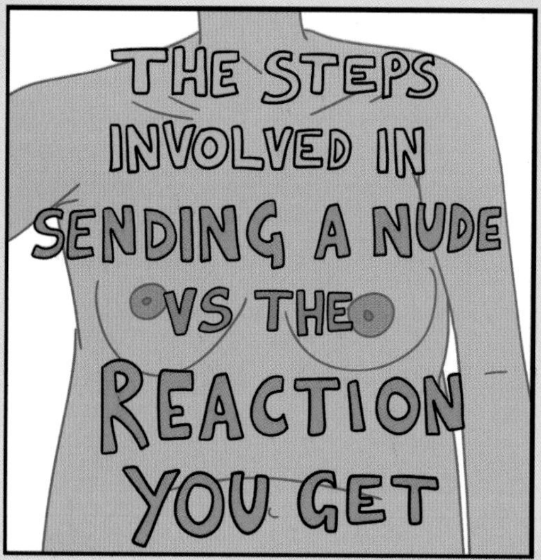
THE STEPS INVOLVED IN SENDING A NUDE VS THE REACTION YOU GET

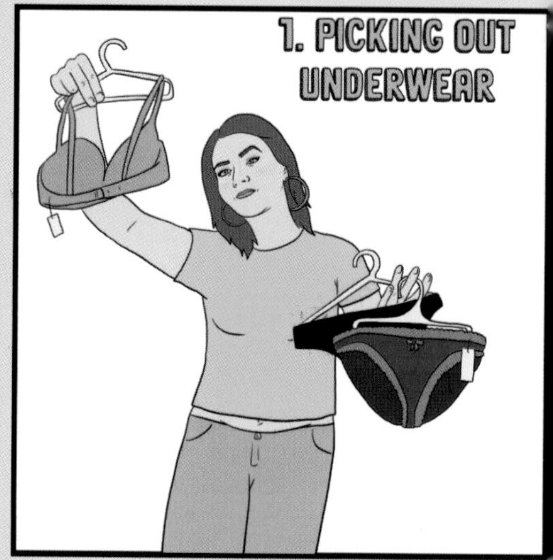
1. PICKING OUT UNDERWEAR

1 of 4

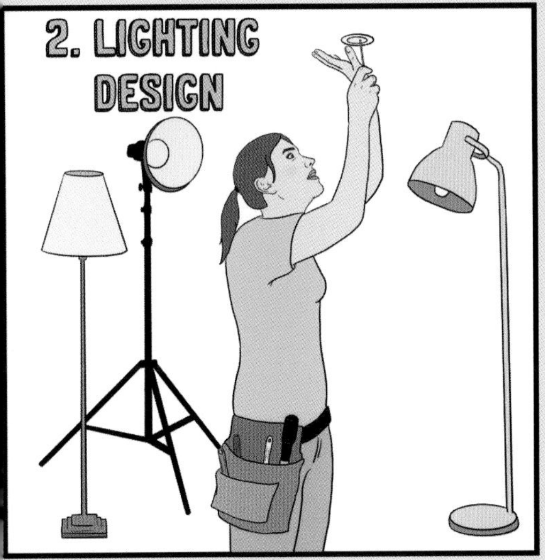
2. LIGHTING DESIGN

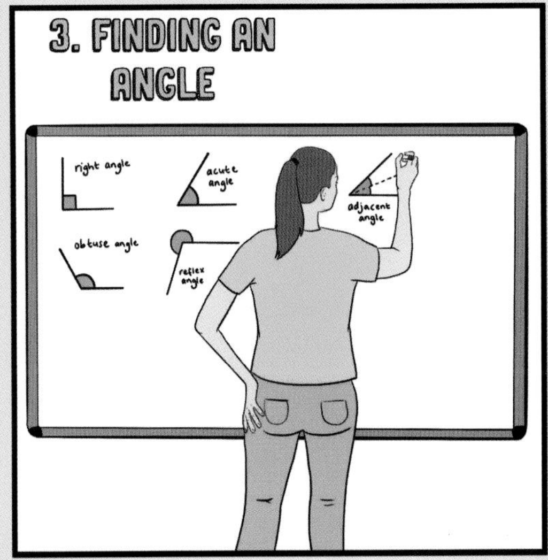
3. FINDING AN ANGLE
right angle
acute angle
adjacent angle
obtuse angle
reflex angle

2 of 4

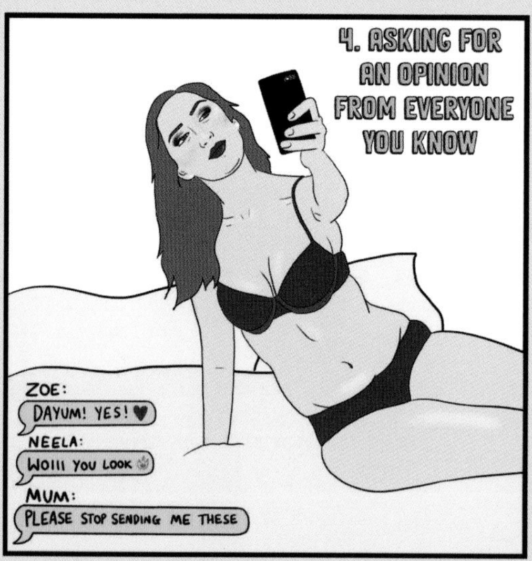
4. ASKING FOR AN OPINION FROM EVERYONE YOU KNOW
ZOE:
DAYUM! YES!
NEELA:
WOIII YOU LOOK
MUM:
PLEASE STOP SENDING ME THESE

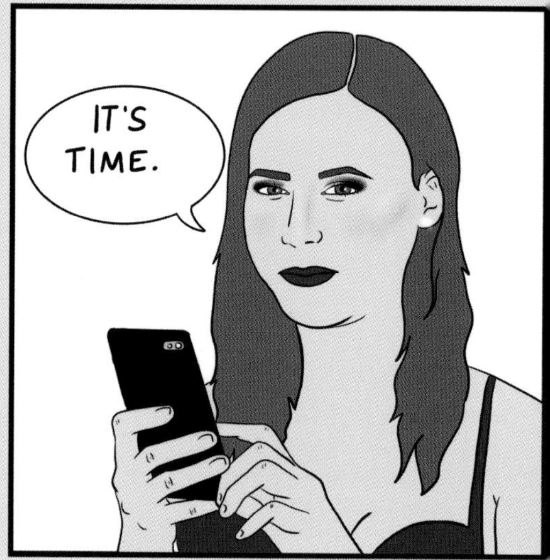
IT'S TIME.

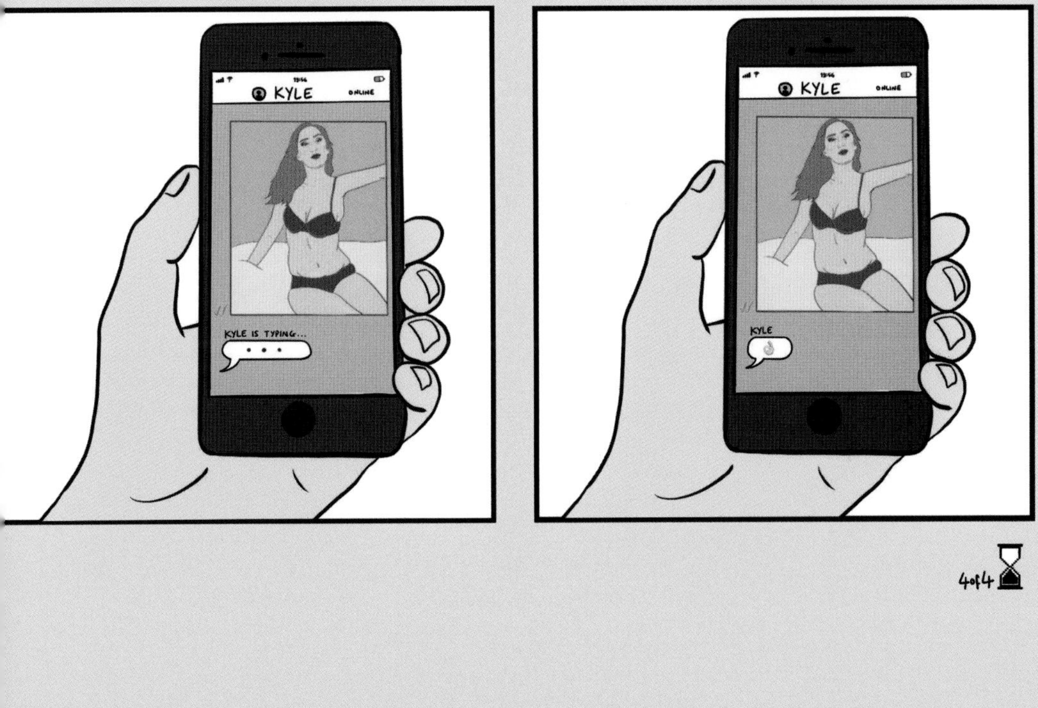
KYLE
ONLINE
KYLE IS TYPING...
KYLE
ONLINE
KYLE

4of4

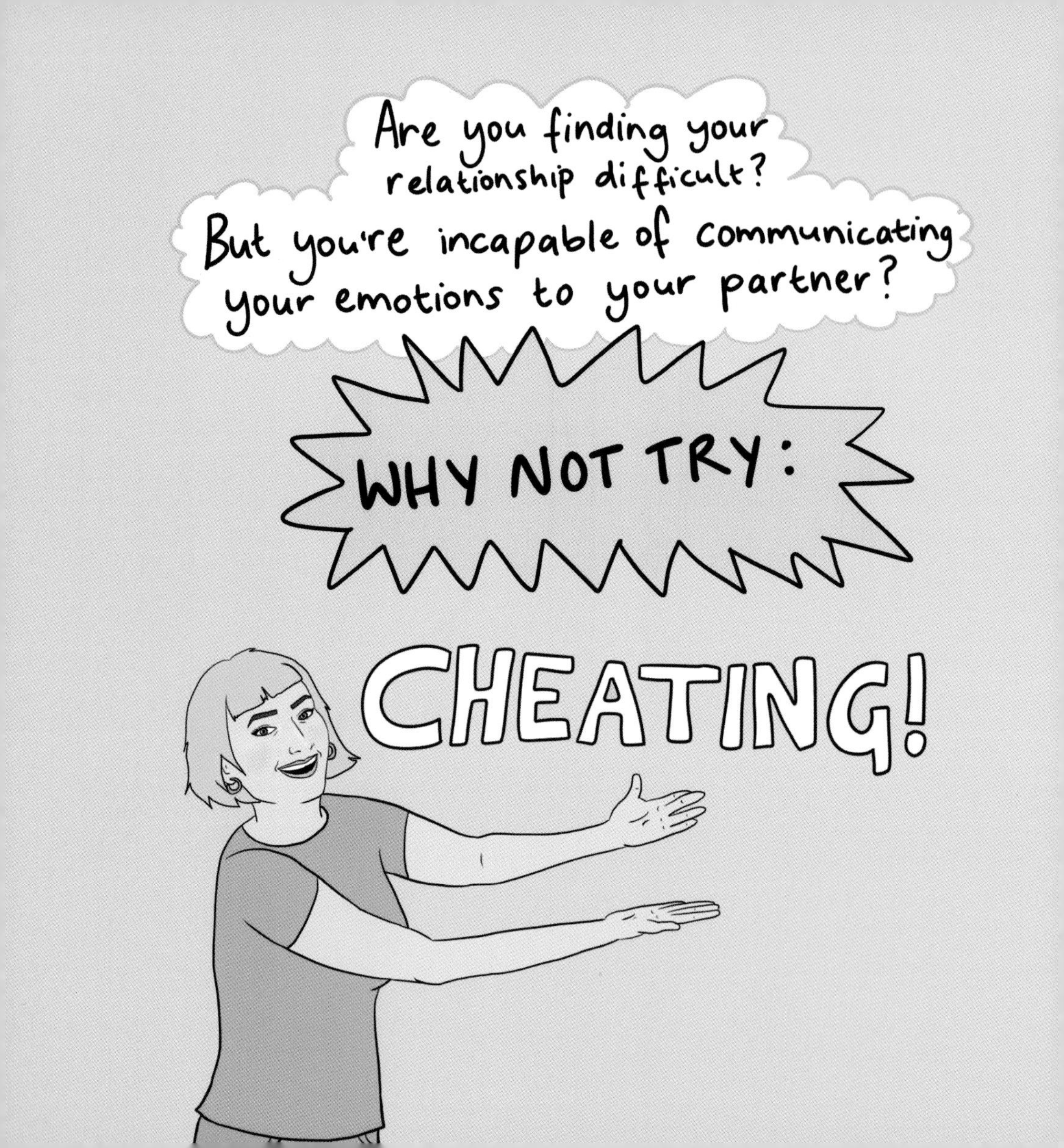
Are you finding your relationship difficult?
But you're incapable of communicating your emotions to your partner?
WHY NOT TRY:
CHEATING!

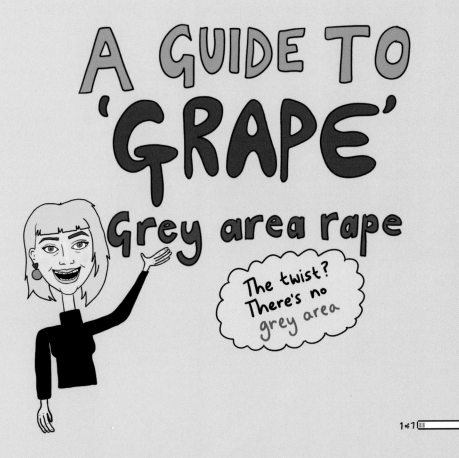

A GUIDE TO 'GRAPE'

Grey area rape

The twist? There's no grey area

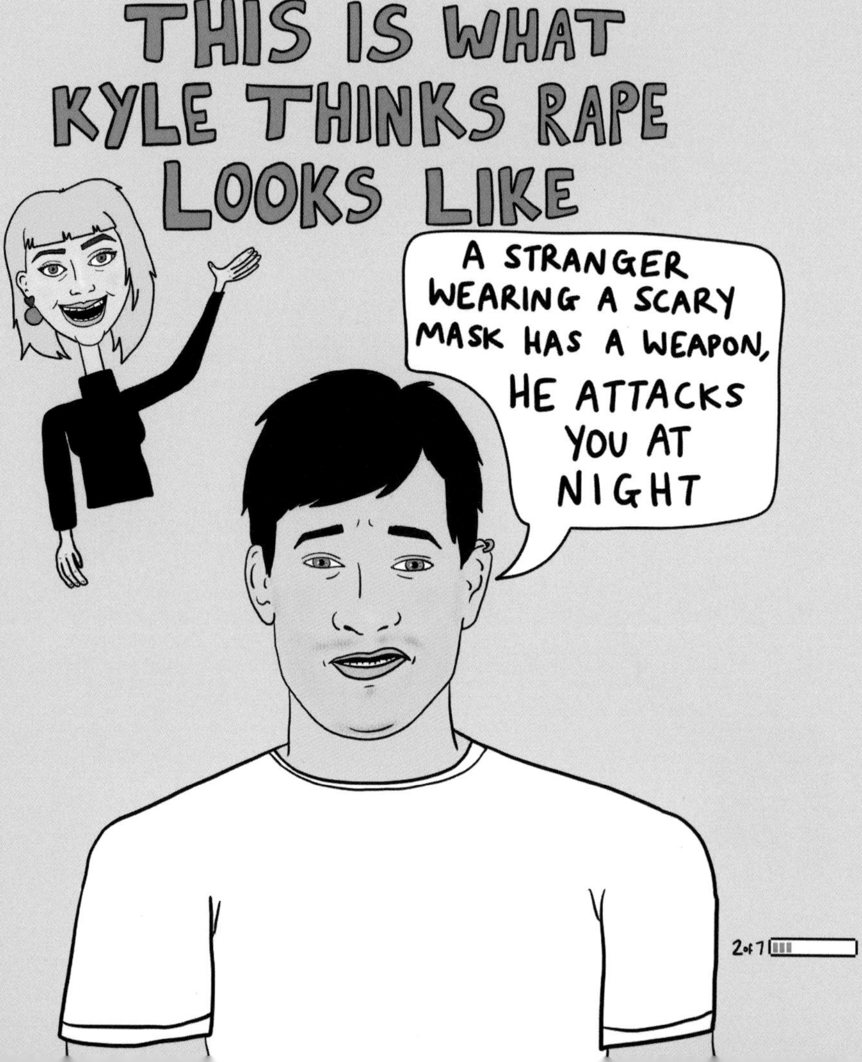
THIS IS WHAT KYLE THINKS RAPE LOOKS LIKE
A STRANGER WEARING A SCARY MASK HAS A WEAPON, HE ATTACKS YOU AT NIGHT
2 of 7

WHY DOES KYLE THINK THIS?

The 'stranger scenario' is predominantly how we learn about rape
3 of 7

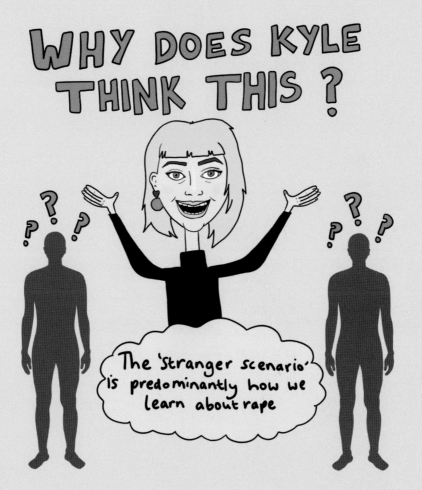

YES

Some attacks do take place within the 'stranger scenario'

BUT

90%

of rape survivors knew their attacker prior to the offence

- family members
- friends
- current partners
- exes
- colleagues

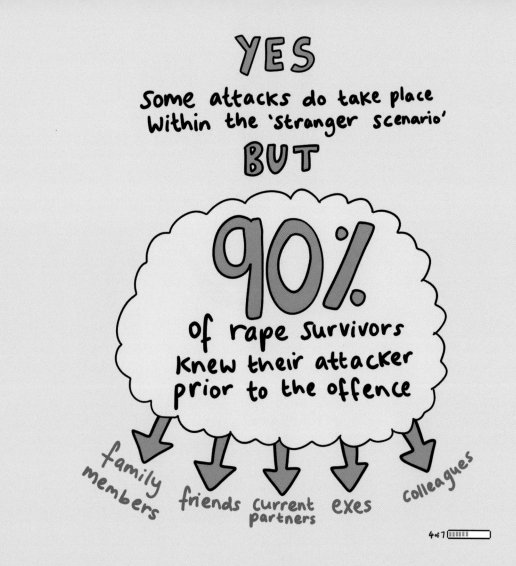

WHAT MAKES PEOPLE THINK THERE ARE GREY AREAS

I was too drunk

We'd been kissing before

He's my friend. He wouldn't have hurt me intentionally

I've had sex with him before

I didn't fight back hard enough

5 of 7

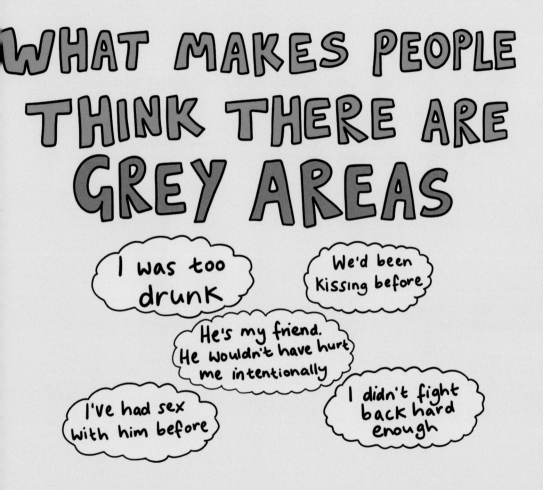

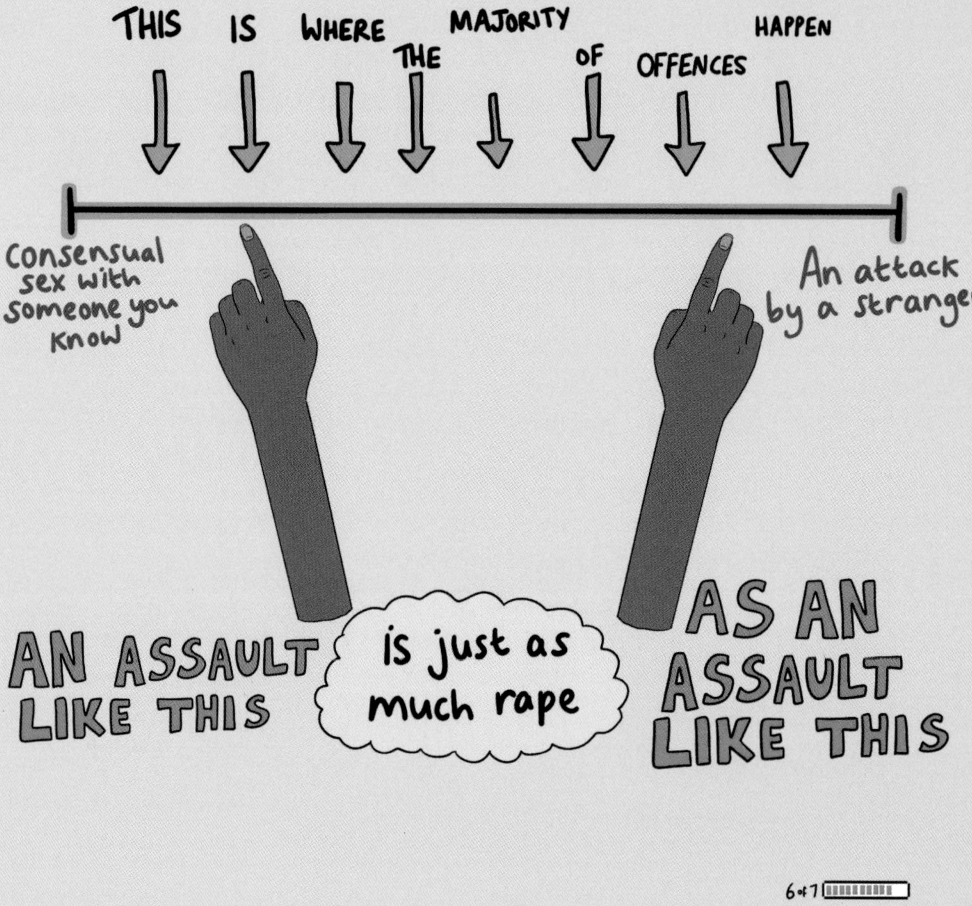
THIS IS WHERE THE MAJORITY OF OFFENCES HAPPEN
Consensual sex with someone you know
An attack by a stranger
AN ASSAULT LIKE THIS
is just as much rape
AS AN ASSAULT LIKE THIS
6 of 7

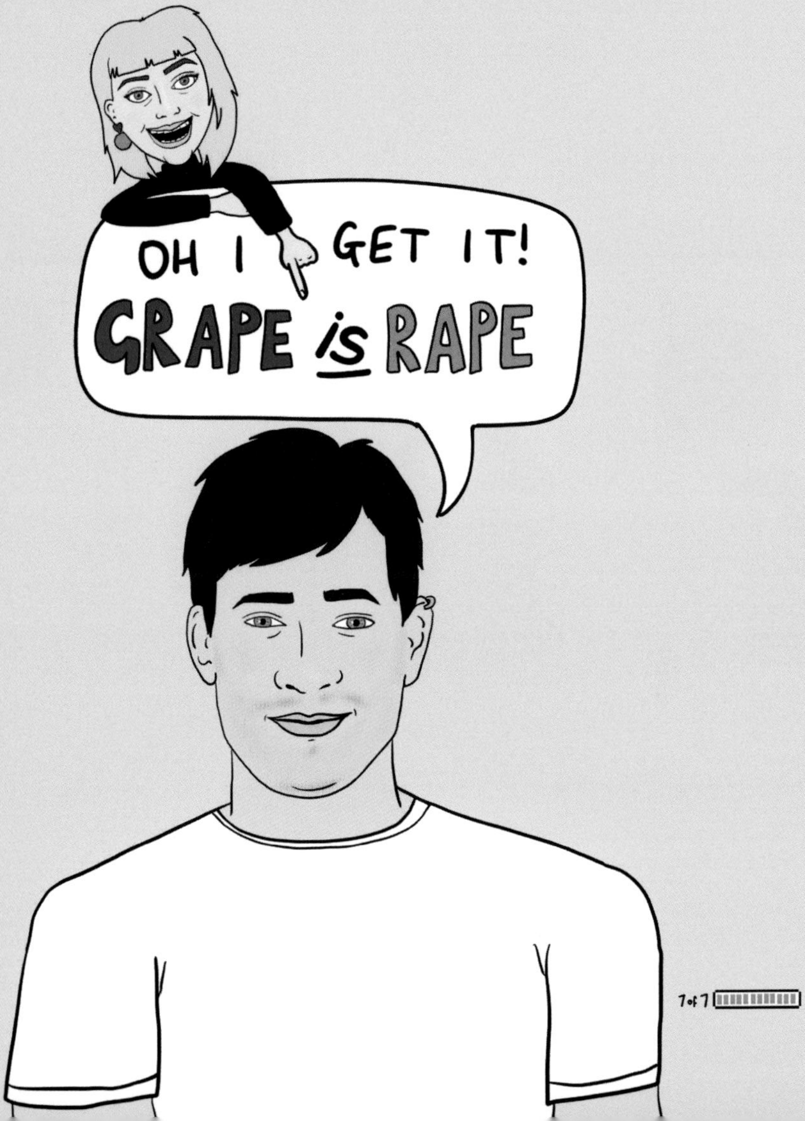
OH I GET IT!
GRAPE is RAPE
7 of 7

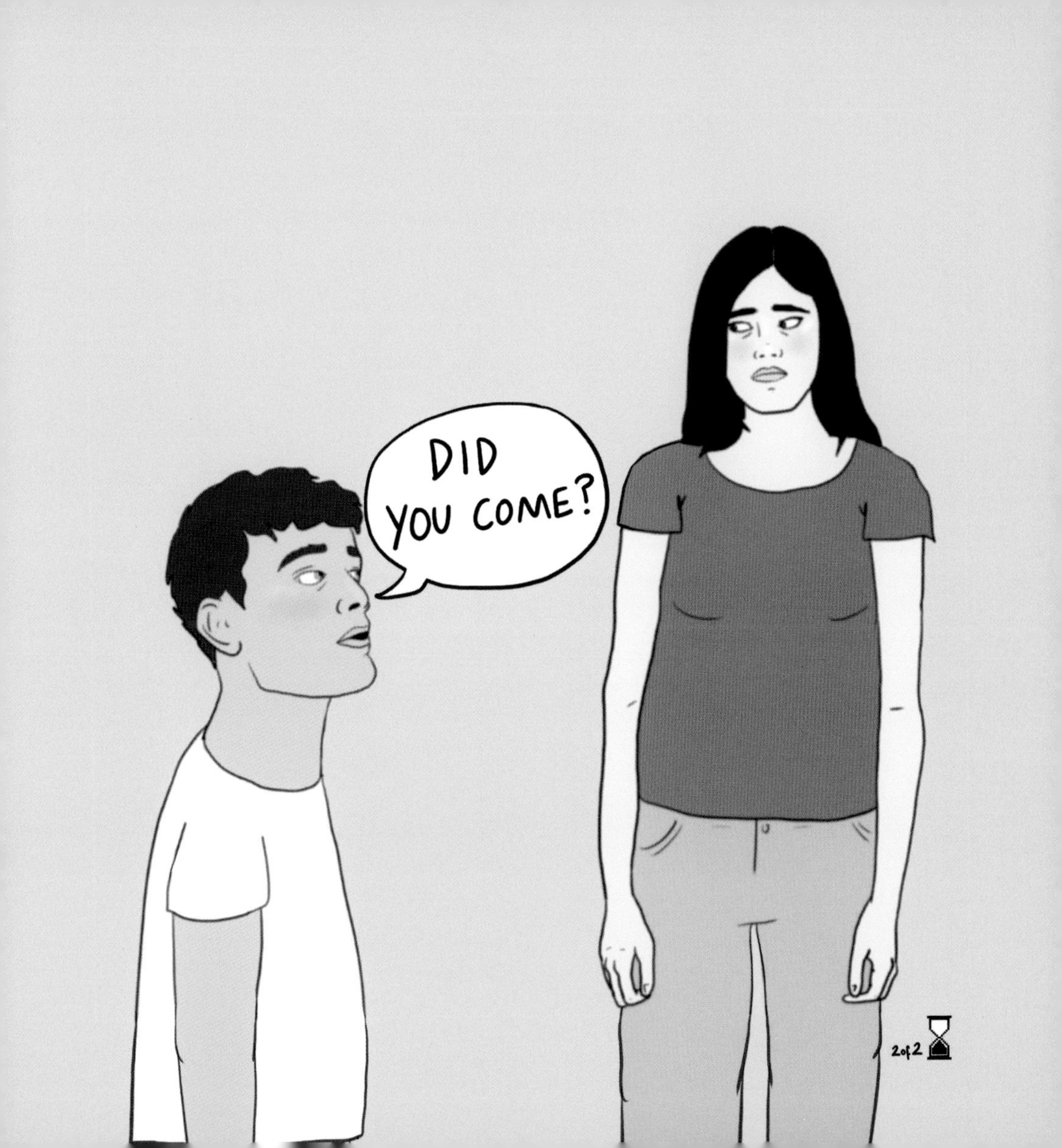
DID YOU COME?
2of2

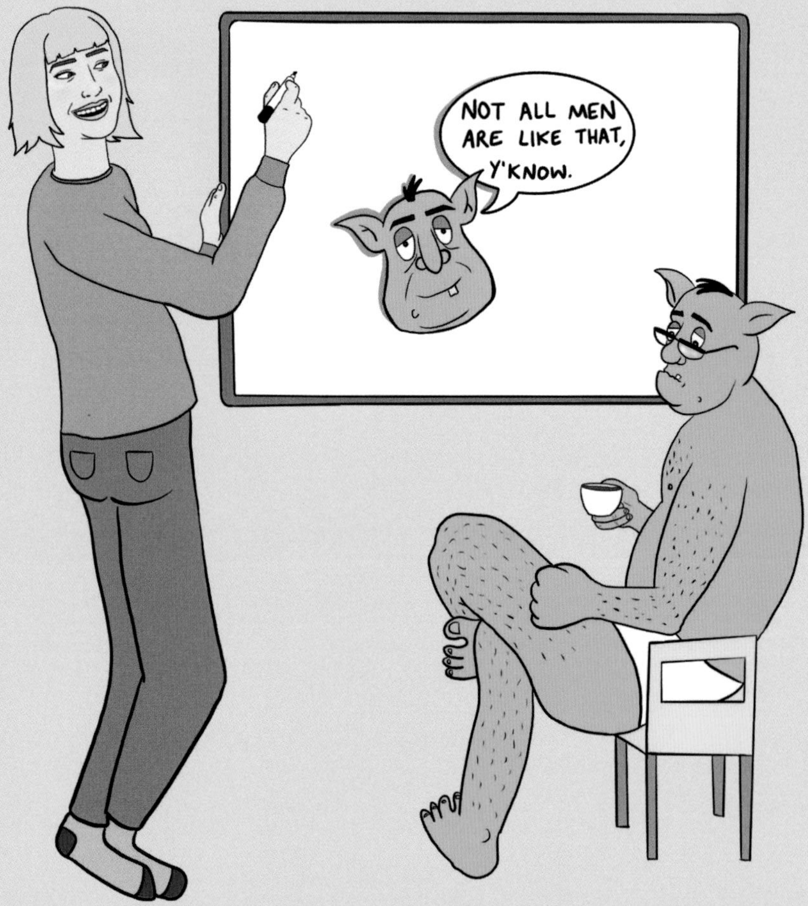
NOT ALL MEN ARE LIKE THAT, Y'KNOW.

NO, NOT ALL MEN ARE LIKE THAT.

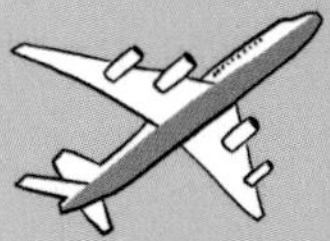

BUT ENOUGH MEN ARE

And even if you're not one of them,
it doesn't mean it's not your problem

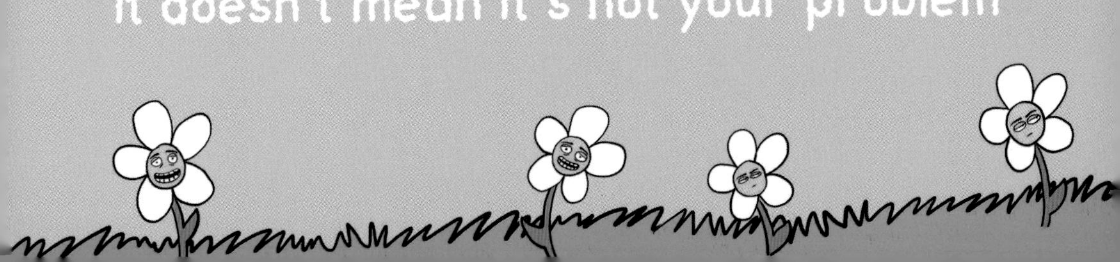

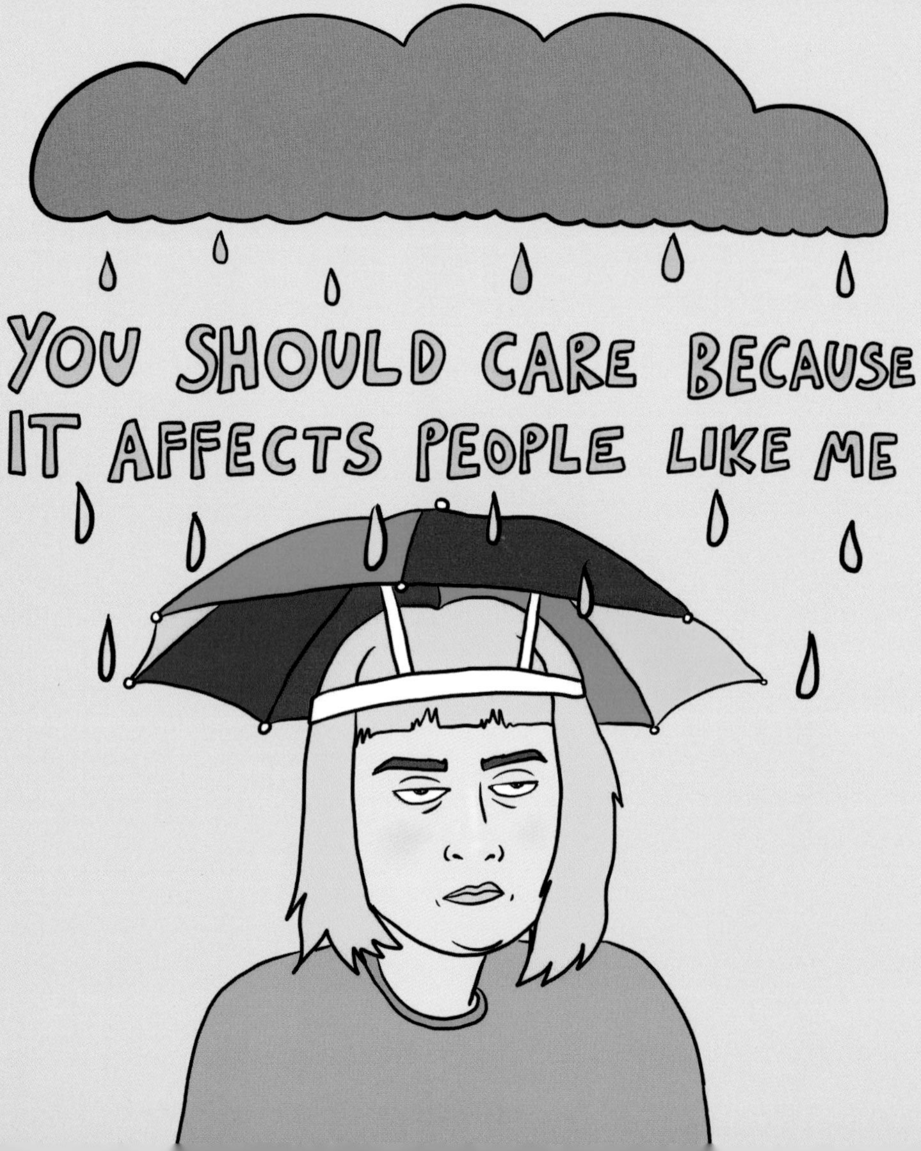
YOU SHOULD CARE BECAUSE
IT AFFECTS PEOPLE LIKE ME

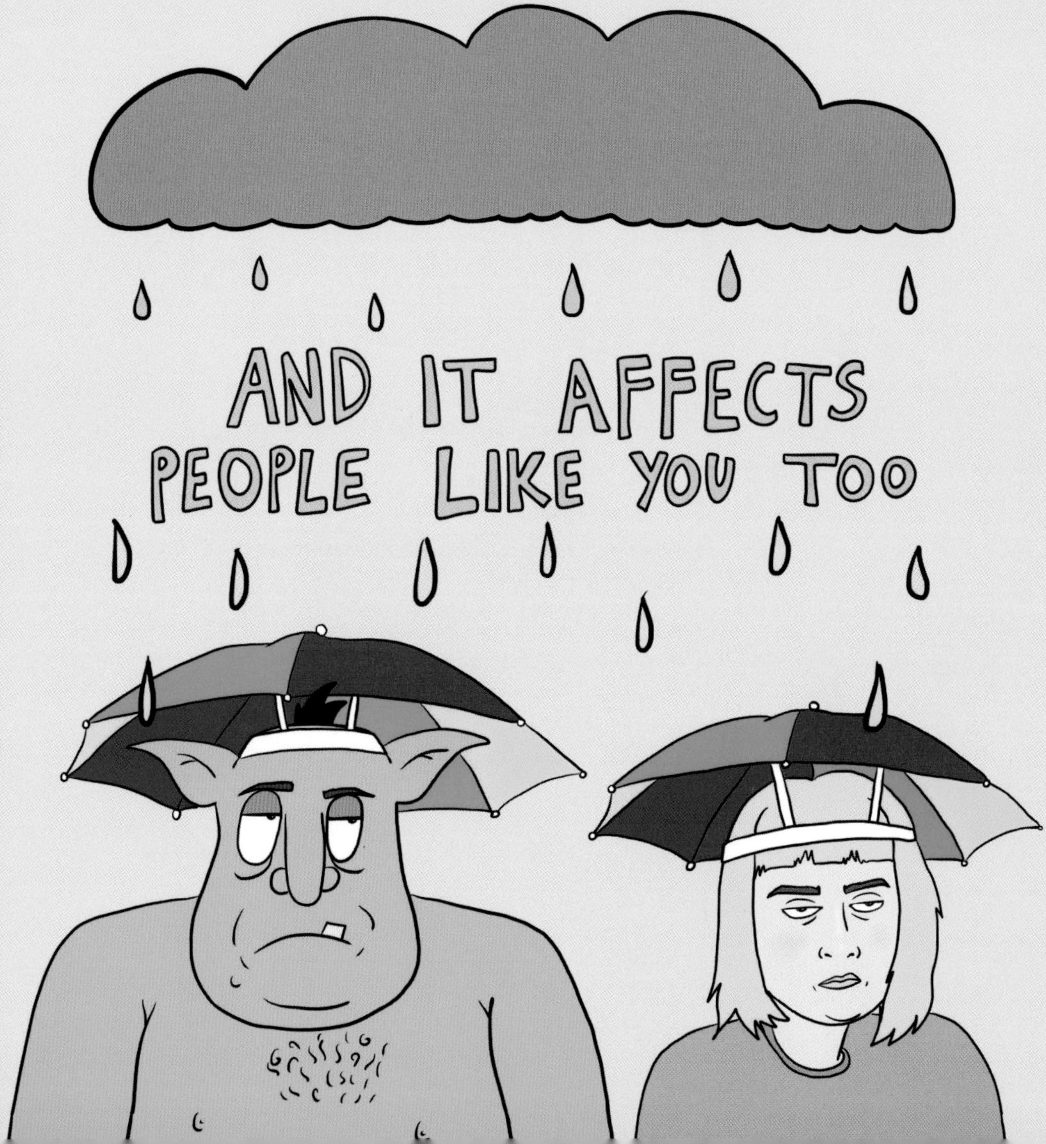
AND IT AFFECTS
PEOPLE LIKE YOU TOO

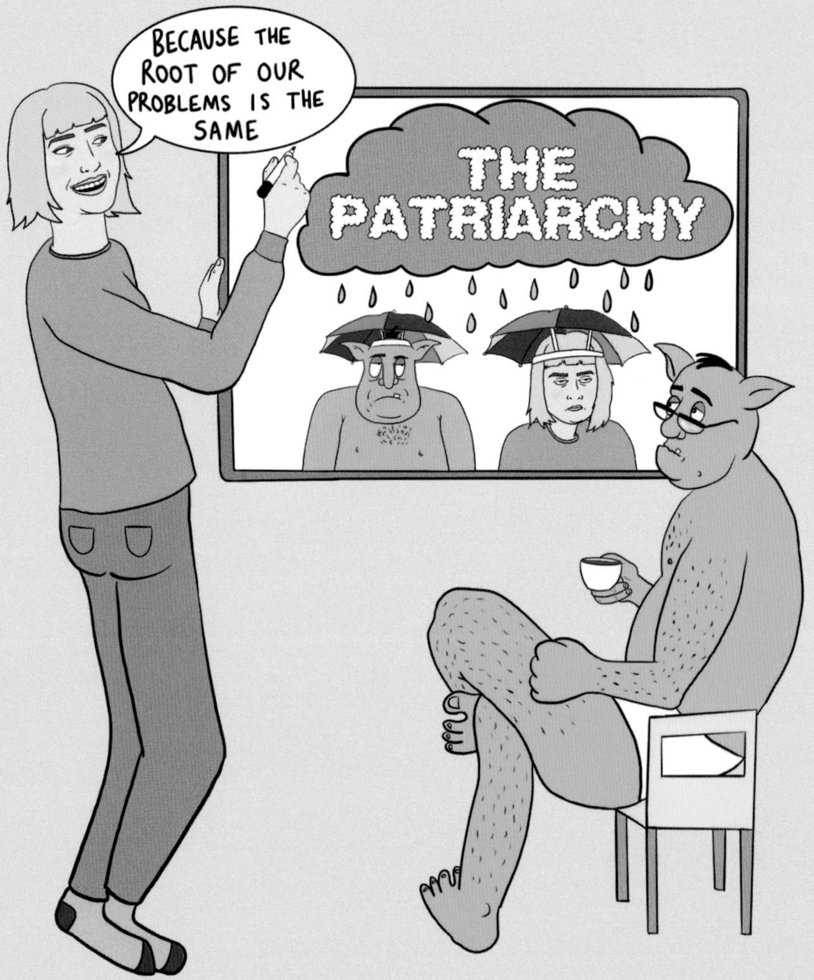
BECAUSE THE ROOT OF OUR PROBLEMS IS THE SAME
THE PATRIARCHY

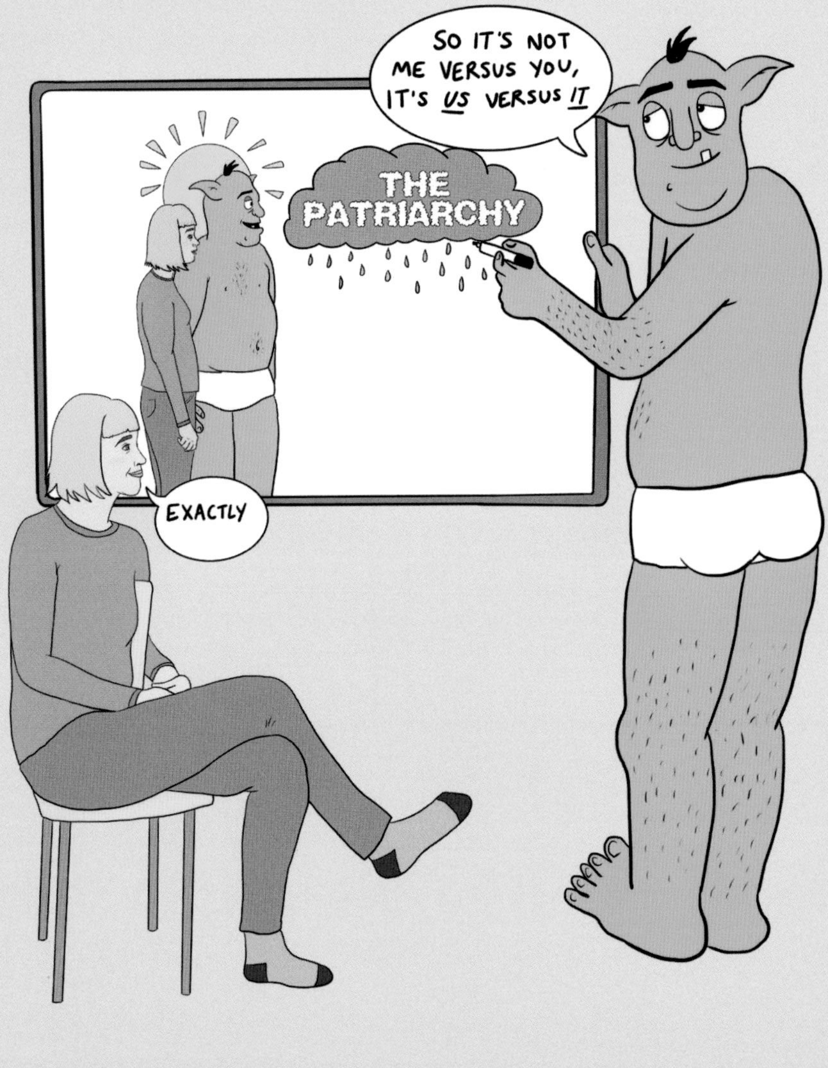
SO IT'S NOT ME VERSUS YOU, IT'S US VERSUS IT
THE PATRIARCHY
EXACTLY

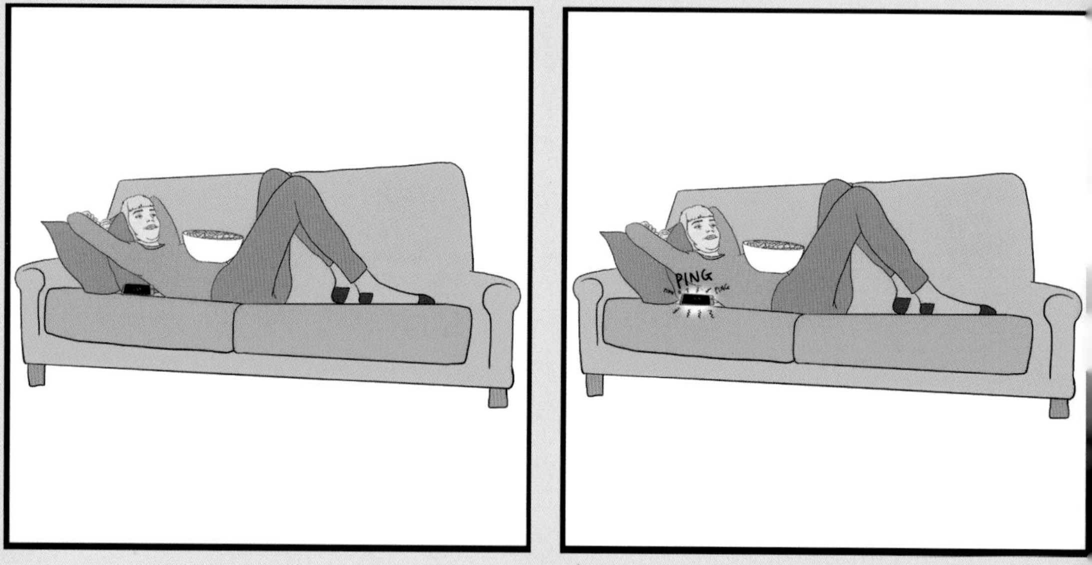
PING
PING

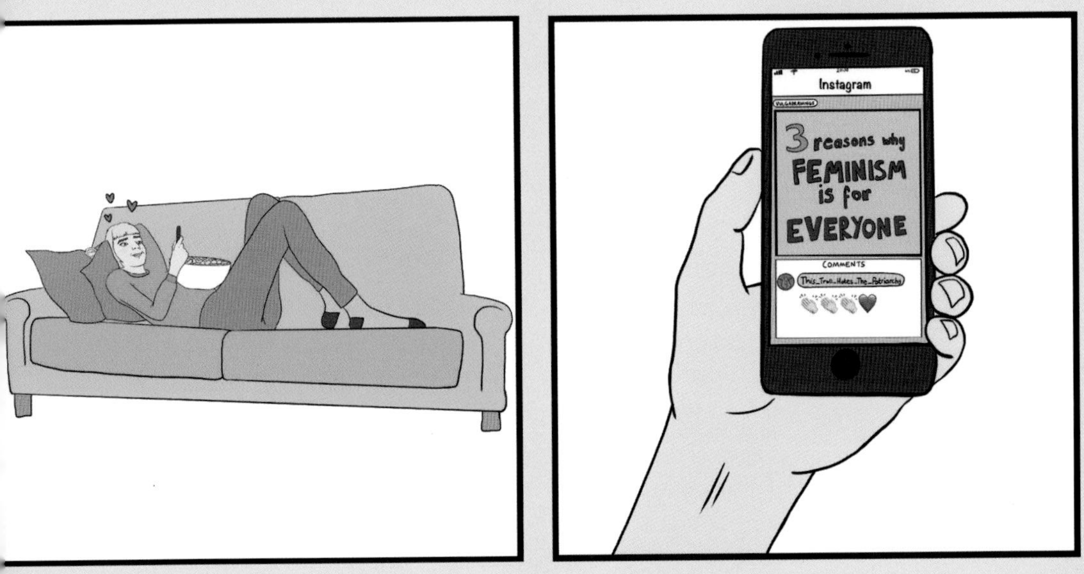
Instagram
3 reasons why FEMINISM is for EVERYONE
COMMENTS
This_Troll_Hates_The_Patriarchy

ABOUT ME

LILY O'FARRELL is a cartoonist from London. She studied sociology at the University of Manchester, has dragged her observations around the London open mic comedy circuit and has been told she has 'an attitude problem' by most of the men who've employed her. In 2017 whilst working as a waitress, she started doodling on the back of receipts (she was a terrible waitress). Since then, she's grown a large online following with her funny drawings about the everyday annoyances of womanhood.

NOT WIFEY MATERIAL

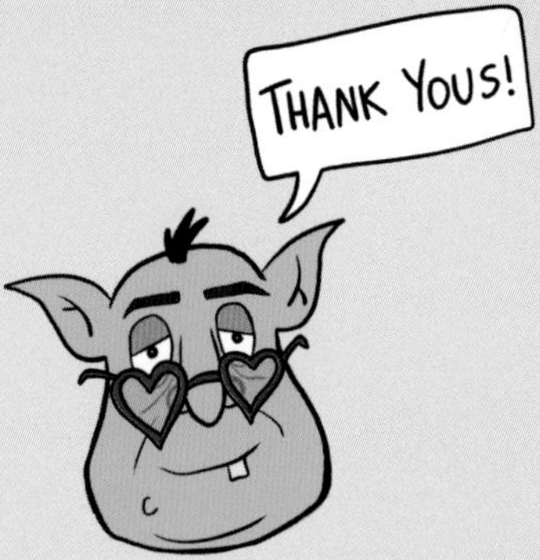
THANK YOUS!

Thank you to my Mum and Dad for their support in me making a living out of what I love, not just making a living to live.

Thank you to the greatest cheerleaders: Jodie, Kathleen, Elsa, Polly, Steph, Bethany, Freddie and Steve.

Thanks to the trolls and everyone who disagrees with me. Most of the time you affirm what I already believe, but sometimes you open my eyes to new ideas.

Thank you to Susie and The Indigo Press for giving me this opportunity and the freedom to do what I want with it.

Shout-out to Susie for her hawk-eyed skill for spotting spelling mistaikes.

Thank you most of all to my Instagram followers, this is without a doubt a team effort.

It's the only group assignment I'd want to be a part of.

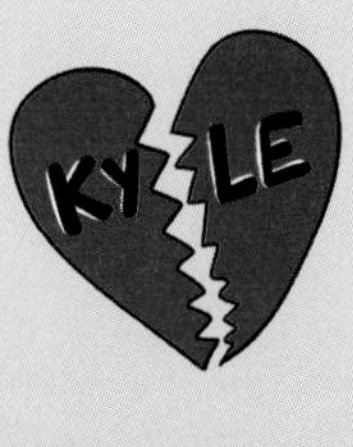
KYLE